The Welfare State Myth

Hobart Paperback 224

About the IEA

Founded in 1955, the Institute of Economic Affairs is Britain's oldest free market think tank. Its mission is to improve understanding of the fundamental institutions of a free society by analysing and expounding the role of markets in solving economic and social problems.

The IEA publishes numerous peer-reviewed books and papers each year as well as shorter briefings. Much of this work is freely available on the IEA website: **www.iea.org.uk**.

The IEA's peer-reviewed academic journal – which it produces with the University of Buckingham, Universidad Francisco Marroquín and Universidad de las Hespérides – is published by Wiley. To receive regular updates on the IEA's work, you can subscribe to our Substack at **insider.iea.org.uk**.

THE WELFARE STATE MYTH

How Low-Tax Countries Offer the World's Best Welfare

STEFAN FÖLSTER
NIMA SANANDAJI

iea
Institute of
Economic Affairs

First published in Great Britain in 2026 by
The Institute of Economic Affairs
2 Lord North Street
Westminster
London SW1P 3LB
in association with London Publishing Partnership Ltd
www.londonpublishingpartnership.co.uk

The mission of the Institute of Economic Affairs is to improve understanding of the fundamental institutions of a free society by analysing and expounding the role of markets in solving economic and social problems.

A CIP catalogue record for this book is available from the British Library.

ISBN 978-0-255-36851-3

Typeset in Kepler by T&T Productions Ltd
www.tandtproductions.com

Printed and bound by Page Bros

CONTENTS

ABOUT THE AUTHORS

Stefan Fölster

Stefan Fölster has been the Chief Economist for the Confederation of Swedish Enterprise, affiliate Professor in Economics at the Royal Institute of Technology in Stockholm and director of the Reform Institute, a think tank based in Stockholm with a focus on innovative reforms. He has authored many academic articles and books, including *Renaissance for Reforms* (co-authored with Nima Sanandaji), published in 2015 by the Institute of Economic Affairs in London. He is also very active in the wider economic discourse with columns and newspaper articles. Two of his other books, co-authored with Dag Detter, are *The Public Wealth of Nations* (Palgrave Macmillan), which was listed among the best books of 2015 in *The Economist* and the *Financial Times*, and *The Public Wealth of Cities*, published in 2017 by the Brookings Institution.

Nima Sanandaji

Dr Nima Sanandaji is an Iranian–Swedish author of Kurdish descent. He has a background in the natural sciences, carrying out some research at the University of California

Santa Barbara, and one year of biotechnology research at the University of Cambridge. He holds two technology PhDs from the Royal Institute of Technology in Stockholm in the field of confined space crystallisation, with some of the research carried out at the University of California Santa Barbara. Dr Sanandaji has published 32 books on the history and evolution of capitalism, healthcare, innovation, entrepreneurship, women's career opportunities, and the future of the Nordic welfare states. He is the president of the think tank ECEPR (European Centre for Entrepreneurship and Policy Reform).

FOREWORD

Before I started working full-time at the IEA, I wrote a dissertation on poverty in developed economies. At the time, the state of the social policy literature was easily summarised. Developed economies could be grouped into three or four different socio-economic models. The clear favourite of the authors was what they called the model of Nordic social democracy, which they described as a restrained form of a market economy where high, progressive taxes fund generous, encompassing and universal welfare states. Their *bête noir*, on the other hand, was what they called the model of neoliberal or Anglo-Saxon capitalism, of which they saw the US as the purest example. This was described as an almost unrestrained form of capitalism, where low taxes fund only a minimalistic, stringently means-tested welfare state.

There was some acknowledgement that, purely in terms of economic outcomes, the latter system had a slight edge. GDP per capita was higher in America than in Sweden or Denmark. (Norway, with its oil wealth, was a bit of a special case.) In terms of social outcomes, however, the (presumed) Nordic model was presented as vastly superior. The implication was that Americans paid a very high human price for a few extra dollars of GDP. There was an acknowledgement of an equity–efficiency trade-off of a sort, but it was presented as essentially a no-brainer. Moving from the low-tax/small-state end of the spectrum to the high-tax/big-state end would entail minimal losses in economic output in exchange for vast social gains.

The rest of the developed world was presumed to be somewhere in between. The UK was presented as more American (with the NHS as a redeeming feature), Germany and the Netherlands as more Scandinavian.

One could find more scholarly versions of this idea in the academic literature. One could find simpler, more openly political versions in the publications of international organisations such as UNICEF, and in the campaign materials of left-wing charities such as Oxfam or the Child Poverty Action Group. At its most basic, it was the subject of countless *Guardian* articles, where it was boiled down to 'Sweden good, America bad'. *The Spirit Level*, probably the most influential political book of the period, tapped into it as well. (Although the authors did not see themselves as 'Big Government' advocates: their aim was equality, and they said they were agnostic with regard to how it was achieved.)

This was the conventional wisdom at the time. The market economy, the thinking went, can produce material wealth, but it cannot provide any of the other things that we value, such as poverty relief, social inclusion, education, affordable housing or healthcare (let alone immaterial goods such as fairness or community cohesion). The market economy can produce material wealth, but everything else has to be provided by the state. The larger and more encompassing the state, the better the social outcomes will be, and if this leads to a high tax burden, that is a price more than worth paying.

I did not find it terribly persuasive even at the time. For a start: is the size of the welfare state really the only difference between America and Sweden? Would America really be just like Sweden if they adopted a Nordic-style welfare state?

And why focus so much on this small sample of countries? It was quite clear that this pattern did not hold across the board. There were other welfare states of near-Scandinavian proportions which failed to produce anything like Scandinavian social outcomes, and there were welfare states much smaller than the American one which did not experience America's social problems.

Nonetheless, while I had my doubts, I could see where people were getting the idea from. It really was quite remarkable how often the Nordic countries topped ranking lists of social indicators. They were quite clearly doing something right. My impression was that the standard social policy literature was not telling the full story, but my impression was not that the literature was completely wrong, or baseless.

The term 'replication crisis' was not widely used yet: it would take off in the mid 2010s. Today, one wonders how much of the social policy literature would survive a replication check. How much of it was just a fluke, based on a snapshot analysis at a particular time?

Quite a lot of it, apparently. In this book, Nima Sanandaji and Stefan Fölster reexamine the relationship between tax levels and social outcomes, using a broad range of social indicators for the latter. Their conclusions differ radically from the conventional wisdom. They find no positive relationship between tax levels and social outcomes whatsoever. It is quite often the comparatively low-tax/small-state models which excel when it comes to social performance, and it is often the high-tax/big-state models which struggle.

The authors make it very clear that they are *not* claiming that there is a causal relationship here. They are explicitly *not* saying that low taxes 'cause' positive social outcomes, or that high taxes 'cause' negative social outcomes. The only times that they mention causality at all, it is in reference to relationships established elsewhere in the economic literature.

The claim they make is a much more modest one. It is that it is *possible* to achieve positive social outcomes without a large state, and that a large state *does not guarantee* positive social outcomes. For this more modest claim, showing correlations is good enough: demonstrating causal relationships is not necessary. They describe various plausible mechanisms that *might* explain why high-tax nations often fail to achieve their desired goals, but that is as far as they will go, and no further.

Nonetheless, even without a causality claim, this book is a game-changer that casts serious doubt on the conventional wisdom.

Proponents of the conventional wisdom are not simply saying that, other things equal, progressive taxation and comprehensive welfare provision improve social outcomes somewhat, compared to what they would otherwise be. They claim, or at least heavily imply, that the size of the welfare state is *the* key determinant of social outcomes. This is a much stronger claim, which is therefore more open to challenge.

In this book, Nima Sanandaji and Stefan Fölster are finally providing that long-overdue challenge. The conventional wisdom does not come out well.

KRISTIAN NIEMIETZ
Editorial Director, Institute of Economic Affairs
May 2025

SUMMARY

Welfare is a broad term, which in public policy tends to refer to deliverance and quality of important services such as healthcare, education, support to vulnerable groups and various systems to create inclusion in the labour market. Welfare is important because most people want to live in societies which take good care of the young, the sick, the poor and the elderly. Central, regional and municipal governments struggle to ensure high-quality welfare services. For decades it was a truism that countries such as the Nordics with generous state-run welfare services succeeded best, although not everyone was convinced that it was worth the high tax take.

This book now reveals a remarkable shift. A group of low-tax countries has moved to the top in terms of most measures of welfare quality, surpassing high-tax countries such as the Nordics. This is relevant, not least since for a long time the Nordic high-tax models were considered internationally as the best model for welfare delivery. Yet even the Nordic social and economic success was built during periods of low taxes, and stagnated in relative terms after shifting to high taxes. This development is analysed here and interpreted with the aid of a new theory of *welfare state crowding out*. Countries which too readily resort to tax increases in order to finance further expansions of the welfare state easily waste resources on extravagances, or neglect efficiency. Eventually, this crowds out some of the most essential welfare state tasks. High taxes and excessive income support also crowd out market welfare services, precautionary saving and insurances as well as the role of the family.

At the core of this book is a systematic analysis of the available statistical measures that capture the quality of welfare in higher-income countries. These measures range from broad indicators, such as life expectancy, to specific metrics such as the number of preventable errors in healthcare or OECD's PISA[1] scores of educational outcomes. PISA is an international survey of the knowledge of 9th graders,[2] which allows for a better understanding of weaknesses, strengths and developments of various nations' education models. It is the best available international measure, and widely used for analysis. Countries with an average tax burden of up to 35 per cent of GDP over a decade are defined as being low tax, those with a tax burden between 35 and 40 per cent defined as medium-tax countries, and those with a tax burden of above 40 per cent are defined as high-tax countries.

A first, comprehensive, analysis shows that a number of low-tax countries now have better welfare outcomes in most areas. This overall ranking is based on 12 measures available over time from the World Bank and the OECD

1 Programme for International Student Assessment (https://www.oecd.org/en/about/programmes/pisa.html).

2 At age 14–15, children in formal education are in the 9th grade in the US and in Year 10 in the UK.

for 23 developed countries in the four areas of health, education, labour markets and social exclusion.

Second, the comprehensive comparison is supported by more detailed analysis using specific metrics, which are not always available for all countries. Along the way, case examples are introduced. This renders a description of how some of the most successful countries have organised their welfare systems. Finally, the results are structured within the framework of a new theory of welfare state crowding out.

In the overall ranking, Switzerland, Japan and South Korea occupy the top spots. All of these are low-tax countries, with a tax burden between 26 and 32 per cent of GDP. By comparison, a high-tax country like Sweden now ranks 12th in terms of overall welfare, in the middle among the included countries. The tax take in Sweden is 43 per cent of GDP.

The perception of the Nordics as having superior welfare was formed several decades ago. Around 1970 Sweden was particularly admired when it had among the highest incomes per capita in the world and was transitioning from low to high taxes. That year, Sweden also had the highest life expectancy in a comparison of 23 wealthy countries but has since slipped to 8th place. Instead, the low-tax nations Japan, South Korea, Australia, Ireland and New Zealand have all climbed into the top-ten league of countries.

Low taxes are not sufficient on their own to ensure good welfare outcomes. Low-tax countries such as the US or Spain do poorly in terms of welfare quality. The

UK is also a low-tax country according to our definition, although if current trends of tax hikes continue it might soon be a medium-tax country. Currently, the UK ranks low on many measures of welfare quality, with the exception of the quality of education. On average, however, when comparing all 23 developed economies, countries with lower taxes now tend to achieve better outcomes.

Raising taxes to better fund welfare has been a staple of political discourse, yet data show that successful low-tax models such as Ireland, Australia or New Zealand can have better outcomes. One implication is that low-tax countries that currently suffer weaker welfare quality such as the US and to some extent the UK could potentially improve welfare drastically without raising taxes.

In health, low-tax countries also lead with longer life expectancy and more hospital beds per capita. A review of healthcare quality measures confirms that some low-tax countries such as Switzerland or Japan often rank best. This is also true for detailed measures such as so-called 'avoidable mortality', defined as deaths that could have been prevented with better medical treatment and preventive care. High-tax countries such as Sweden seem to do reasonably well in some healthcare quality measures, but are not the best, and suffer from long waiting times, fewer doctor visits despite a relatively high number of doctors per capita, and dissatisfaction among patients with brief consultation times and poor handling of information.

Education results in terms of various PISA measures are better in low-tax countries on average. A leading star is Estonia, but the UK also does fairly well. A key part of the new *welfare state crowding out theory* relates to the fact that pupils, parents and teachers are all influenced by how high the reward for education is. High-tax countries have lower individual incentives to education, eroding motivation, grit and educational results. This may explain why pupils in Estonia and Ireland now have better PISA results compared to Sweden, for example.

Unemployment tends to be slightly lower in countries with a lower tax burden. For the less educated, unemployment is significantly lower in low-tax countries. The greater effect for less-educated individuals indicates that high-tax models create poverty traps, in which market work is not or just barely more highly rewarded than living on public benefits. This welfare dependency trap can become ingrained in subcultures and persist for generations.

In the area of social exclusion, high-tax countries on average perform slightly better than low-tax countries. However, many low-tax countries still fare better than the iconic welfare states such as Sweden. For instance, in terms of the proportion of the population in material poverty, Switzerland, Iceland and Canada perform significantly better than Sweden, and low-tax countries such as Japan, Ireland and Australia at about the same level.

The welfare state crowding out theory developed in this book does not claim a causal link between taxation and welfare quality but explains the link between high taxes and suboptimal welfare outcomes. During each of the past five decades, real prosperity growth has been higher in countries with low tax rates, making it easier to support good welfare quality. In addition, high-tax countries have tended to waste public funds on unsustainable expansion, poor management and efficiency, poor governance of public assets and poor incentives in social insurance systems, thus crowding out resources that should have gone to the most essential welfare services and to prevention of future social costs. Wasteful practices appear to be more common in countries where many people believe that taxes can always be raised more if deemed necessary.

Against the backdrop of these results the main point of this book is that world-leading welfare quality can be achieved with a considerably smaller tax take than high-tax countries currently spend. Successful low-tax countries will find it much easier to tackle future cost pressures due to an ageing population and other demands on the public purse.

TABLES AND FIGURES

1 MANY COUNTRIES STRUGGLE WITH WELFARE DELIVERY

In economic terms, the word 'welfare' refers to utility, a general term for individual well-being in economic and decision theory. In everyday language, it refers to key services in society such as healthcare, education, support to those in need of economic help, and labour market policies. In all rich countries that are the focus of our comparison, citizens expect governments to guarantee education for the young, healthcare for the sick, aid to those in need, and a functioning labour market and training for those who cannot find work.

Maintaining the quality of welfare services, let alone improving them at the pace that inhabitants ask for, is a challenge for most governments. One good example is analysis of PISA results. PISA is the world-leading test of knowledge of 9th graders. PISA results reveal a long-term decline in educational performance that began in 2009, well before the Covid-19 pandemic. While British pupils remain steadily above average, students in Europe and the US performed poorly in 2022, and significantly worse than in the past, especially in mathematics and reading. If this trend continues, there could be far-reaching social, economic and, in the end, political consequences. Failure at school is often met with more welfare-state support and income redistribution.

The outlook for pensions is also deteriorating. During the past 30 years, the average length of schooling has increased significantly. For example, in Germany and France it was 9.0 and 8.3 years in 1990, respectively. It reached 13.1 and 11.9 years in 2020. Other things equal, if average skills remain the same or deteriorate while the length of schooling is extended, either pensions become smaller, social security contributions must grow or the retirement age is raised.

Healthcare quality is improving in some respects due to technological advance and new treatments. But many countries witness prolonged waiting times. For example, Britain is not yet a high-tax country but it organises its healthcare through a centralised state-run system more typical of high-tax countries. The NHS is the single largest employer in Europe. Hospital waiting lists in England spiralled beyond 7 million in 2024, forcing many to wait months or even years for treatment. Almost 300,000 adults were waiting for a social care assessment. A record 2.5 million Britons were out of work because they were sick. On basic measures of health, Britain suffers by comparison with its rich-world peers. Its people barely live any longer than they did a decade ago and have some of the worst survival rates for diseases such as cancer. Yet in the next 25 years, the number of Britons aged 85 and older is set to double.

The pandemic, climate concerns, the energy crisis and Russia's invasion of Ukraine have overshadowed a more insidious disease: many developed countries are grappling with weaker growth. Between 1980 and 2000, GDP per capita grew by an average of 2.25 per cent per year in the OECD. Since then, growth has shrunk to less than half that figure, only 1.1 per cent per year.

Growth is also more important than ever to provide for an ageing population. Traditionally, economists often hypothesised that an aging population could only be supported with a larger share of the workforce employed in elder care and healthcare, funded through higher taxes. Instead, it is now becoming clear that the anticipated waves of new employees in the welfare sector are hard to attract, and even if it were possible, voters have limited interest in higher taxes. Instead, growing demand for welfare services must be addressed by better organisation and investments in smarter technology and infrastructure. A country can only afford such investments if the economy grows.

While most countries struggle to maintain welfare quality, some do relatively well. The remarkable shift shown in detail in later chapters is already apparent in one of the earliest and most basic metrics of welfare quality: life expectancy.

Life expectancy mirrors overall welfare trends

A population's life expectancy is the outcome of good governance in several respects, such as policies that provide good material well-being, low crime and traffic accidents, but also the quality of healthcare, education and the prevalence of poverty. Life expectancy at birth is a relevant measure for looking at welfare trends over longer times. Life expectancy at birth is based on the health data of the total current population of different ages. That makes it is a more holistic health measure than, for example, the expected remaining life span at a certain age. Healthy life span is another good alternative measure, but historical analysis over longer times is only possible for total life years since, unlike healthy life years, this has been measured over a longer time and more systematically throughout the world.

Table 1 Life expectancy at birth in 1970 (number of years), rich countries with more than a million adults

1	Sweden	74.6	13	Italy	71.6
2	Norway	74.1	14	New Zealand	71.3
3	Iceland	73.9	15	Australia	71.0
4	Netherlands	73.6	16	Belgium	71.0
5	Denmark	73.3	17	Ireland	70.9
6	Switzerland	73.0	18	US	70.8
7	Greece	72.8	19	Germany	70.4
8	Canada	72.7	20	Finland	70.2
9	Spain	72.0	21	Austria	69.9
10	UK	72.0	22	Portugal	67.1
11	Japan	71.9	23	South Korea	62.2
12	France	71.7			

Half a century ago, the Nordic countries topped the list for life expectancy at birth – but they had not yet become high-tax countries. Even other European countries such as the UK were among the top ten. Table 1 shows life expectancy at birth in 1970.

By 2020 the picture had changed considerably. Low-tax countries dominate at the top. Of the ten countries with the highest life expectancy, eight are low-tax countries.

Sweden has fallen from first to eighth position. Other high-tax countries such as Belgium and Denmark have also fallen. France, which has become a high-tax country, remains in 12th place.

Table 2 Life expectancy at birth in 2020 (number of years), rich countries with more than a million adults

1	Japan	84.6	Climbed in rank (low-tax country)
2	South Korea	83.4	Climbed in rank (low-tax country)
3	Norway	83.2	
4	Australia	83.2	Climbed in rank (low-tax country)
5	Iceland	83.1	
6	Switzerland	83.0	
7	Ireland	82.6	Climbed in rank (low-tax country)
8	Sweden	82.4	Fell in rank (high-tax country)
9	Spain	82.3	
10	New Zealand	82.3	Climbed in rank (low-tax country)
11	Italy	82.2	
12	France	82.2	
13	Finland	81.9	Climbed in rank (high-tax country)
14	Canada	81.7	Fell in rank (low-tax country)
15	Denmark	81.6	Fell in rank (high-tax country)
16	Netherlands	81.4	Fell in rank (medium-tax country)
17	Greece	81.3	Fell in rank (medium-tax country)
18	Austria	81.2	
19	Germany	81.0	
20	Portugal	81.0	
21	Belgium	80.7	Fell in rank (high-tax country)
22	UK	80.4	Fell in rank (low-tax country)
23	US	77.0	Fell in rank (low-tax country)

This development provides an indication of the results that follow in later chapters in this book. It is not the case that all low-tax countries have the best welfare outcomes. The US, for example, ends up at the bottom of Table 2 with a relatively low life expectancy. The UK, also a low-tax country, has fallen from 10th to 22nd position. However, systematic comparisons in the coming chapters show that on average countries with low taxes have succeeded best. Welfare outcomes in terms of health are not just about the healthcare system, they are influenced by how society at large functions, as well as lifestyle factors. Factors such as obesity and opioid use contribute to why the US has poor health performance (Geloso 2023).

The experience of the Nordic countries is particularly illuminating since they were once seen as a paradigm for high-quality welfare services.

The example of the Nordics

Sweden has long received international attention for its remarkable development from a poor country to one of the richest during the hundred years between 1870 and 1970. Yet it was only in the1970s that Sweden raised taxes to levels above most other European countries and opened the taps of state welfare systems. In the mid 1960s, the tax rate was just over 31 per cent. As late as 1968, Sweden was still a low-tax economy, with a tax ratio just under 35 per cent of economic output. When Swedish life expectancy was at its peak compared to the rest of the world, in 1970, the country had only just raised taxes to over 35 per cent of GDP, which according to our report's definition is a transition to an economy with medium taxes. The foundation for the good growth and success in welfare was thus laid during a period of low taxes (Sanandaji 2015).

For a few years, the country seemed to combine economic success with high taxes and generous welfare. Even researchers were dazzled by this short-lived episode. Most renowned, the sociologist Gøsta Esping-Andersen in 1990 launched a theory in terms of three different forms of what he called 'welfare capitalism' – a liberal welfare regime, a conservative one and a social democratic one with universal welfare systems. The countries that had adopted the latter regime, with a publicly managed welfare sector and extensive tax financing, showed the best results according to a range of welfare measures (Esping-Andersen 1990).

The social democratic welfare regimes are characterised by general social insurance systems under public auspices. Transfers and social insurance are income-related but differ from the conservative regime by 'floors' and 'ceilings' in the allowances. Since social security contributions are collected without a cap, significant redistribution is achieved. Nevertheless, the interests of the middle class are linked to those of the working class by the fact that everyone is part of the same system. In this welfare regime, taxes and benefits are based on individual rather than family earnings, which stimulates women's high labour force participation. Social services are mainly carried out as tax-financed public services, which also implies a significant redistribution. Social policy is redistributive and equalising. Income differences are moderate, especially after taxes and benefits. The social democratic regime was at the time found primarily in the Nordic countries, which also appeared to yield the best welfare outcomes.

In the wake of the shift towards higher taxation, however, Swedish prosperity in relation to the outside world stagnated and the level of ambition in the welfare systems eventually had to be scaled back (Fölster and Sanandaji (2024).

Esping-Andersen's thesis was received with open arms in Sweden by those who wanted to defend all parts of Swedish welfare against critics who pointed to ever more indications that the generous systems were not sustainable. Economic growth was already stagnating from the mid 1970s. Real after-tax incomes did not increase at all during the twenty-year period from the mid 1970s to the mid 1990s. Despite large tax increases to finance welfare – from a tax burden of 38 per cent of GDP in 1970 to 52 per cent in 1990 – public sector debt rose to 80 per cent of GDP. The employment rate appeared to be high but included swelling numbers of people on sick leave. Many were seasonally unemployed and lived on unemployment benefits during the off-season.

Sweden was experiencing welfare state crowding out that culminated in the crisis of the early 1990s. It required a complete overhaul of Swedish economic policy in almost all areas. Welfare systems were adapted to more normal European levels. Housing subsidies, which were previously considered a central part of the welfare state, were largely scrapped. Pensions were reformed and lowered. Unemployment benefits and health insurance were tightened.

After the reforms of the 1990s, growth recovered in Sweden, to such an extent that in 2013 *The Economist* magazine showcased it with a front page: 'Success with a large public sector'. By then the public debt had been largely paid off and the tax burden reduced from 52 per cent to 45 per cent of GDP.

This relative success unfortunately gave rise to a new period of hubris without much interest in efficiency. In recent years, spending has again increased in several welfare areas without a corresponding improvement in performance. At the same time, an investment shortfall has eroded infrastructure, such as the electricity grid, water supply and maintenance of the transport systems. Although the tax burden has been pushed back somewhat, Sweden still belongs to the group of countries with the highest tax burden in the world.

With some variations, the story is similar in other Nordic countries. Denmark is a high-tax country that has fallen in terms of relative welfare quality. Norway has held its own a bit better, largely thanks to enormous oil revenues. Finland was much poorer to start with which allowed a catch-up growth effect. Recently, this has slowed considerably and cracks in welfare delivery are starting to show. For example, Finland had been a leader in terms of school quality, but has in recent years seen falling results after also remodelling its school system more in line with the one in Sweden and many other high-tax countries.

Against the background of Nordic experiences, what is the general pattern connecting welfare quality and taxes? That is the subject of the following chapters.

2 SYSTEMATIC ANALYSIS: COUNTRIES WITH LOWER TAX BURDENS TEND TO HAVE BETTER WELFARE OUTCOMES

This chapter provides a comprehensive comparison of welfare quality, while later chapters dive into various areas, based on more specific measures and descriptions of how some countries manage to get good results with lower public spending and other countries spend a lot but get worse results.

A total of twelve welfare measures divided into four areas are shown, selected because they are central measures of welfare outcomes (rather than inputs or entitlements) and available for many countries over several decades. The data are obtained from the World Bank's World Development Indicators and the OECD's PISA surveys.

The four areas are: health, education, unemployment and exclusion. Within each area, three of the most important measures have been included in the analysis that were also available for all countries over several decades. Together, they arguably capture much of what welfare systems aim to achieve. Later sections also show that the trends of low-tax countries' better welfare outcomes are also reflected in more detailed statistics.

Each welfare category contains three dimensions. The unemployment category includes, for example, unemployment for those with low, medium and high levels of education. To avoid being misled by annual fluctuations, average outcomes since 2010 form the basis for the analysis. For each measure the relative ranking of countries is calculated. The country that has the worst outcome in a measure gets a grade of 1, while the country that has the best outcome gets a grade of 10; the others are then graded based on the distance between the bottom and the top.

As an illustration, South Korea averaged 2.7 per cent low-skilled unemployment for the years since 2010, the lowest level of all countries. This gives the country a score of 10. In Spain, the level was the highest, 26 per cent. The country thus receives a rating of 1. Sweden has 20 per cent unemployment among the low educated and receives a rating of 3.4, which indicates that the country is closer to the bottom than the top. Overall, for the dimension of unemployment, however, Sweden receives a grade of 6.9, because the level of unemployment among the medium and highly educated is relatively low. In these two cases, Sweden is closer to the top than the bottom.

The formula for each measure is:

$$I_i = 1 + \left(9\frac{x_i - m_0}{m - m_0}\right)$$

where I_i is the normalised index for country i, x_i is the observed value of the indicator for that country, m_0 is the minimum goalpost (i.e. the lowest value for the indicator among compared countries) and m is the maximum goalpost (i.e. the highest value among the 23 countries in the comparison). This formulation ensures that each indicator is expressed on a common scale from 1 to 10, where 1 corresponds to the minimum and 10 to the maximum.

Table 3 Advanced countries ranked after outcome in average for four welfare dimensions

		Welfare (a)	*Unemployment (b)*	*Health (c)*	*Education (d)*	*Exclusion (e)*	*Tax burden (f)*
1	Japan	9.4	9.6	9.5	10.0	8.6	30
2	South Korea	8.0	9.7	7.5	9.2	5.6	26
3	Switzerland	7.5	8.8	6.4	6.7	8.0	27
4	Norway	7.4	9.3	6.6	4.7	9.1	40
5	Germany	7.4	8.9	6.5	5.4	8.8	38
6	Australia	7.2	8.4	6.2	6.8	7.5	27
7	Austria	7.0	8.4	6.4	5.7	7.4	42
8	Denmark	7.0	8.2	4.8	6.2	8.8	46
9	New Zealand	6.9	8.7	4.7	6.6	7.6	32
10	Netherlands	6.9	8.8	5.5	5.0	8.3	38
11	Belgium	6.7	7.6	5.9	5.7	7.6	43
12	Sweden	6.7	6.9	5.7	5.9	8.3	43
13	Finland	6.7	6.8	5.2	6.6	8.0	43
14	Iceland	6.5	9.1	6.5	2.0	8.5	36
15	UK	6.5	8.3	4.3	6.5	6.9	33
16	Ireland	6.4	6.3	5.2	7.5	6.6	24
17	Canada	6.4	7.0	4.1	7.7	6.9	33
18	France	6.3	6.6	6.1	5.0	7.6	45
19	US	5.7	8.1	1.1	6.2	7.2	25
20	Italy	5.3	6.7	6.0	4.9	3.7	43
21	Portugal	5.2	6.4	4.1	4.9	5.4	34
22	Spain	4.7	2.4	6.4	4.9	5.2	34
23	Greece	2.4	1.6	5.5	1.1	1.5	38

(a) Average for four welfare dimensions; (b) dimension unemployment; (c) dimension health; (d) dimension education; (e) dimension exclusion; (f) taxes as share of GDP (%), average since 2010.

Sources: Data on outcomes in unemployment, health and exclusion are different indicators from the World Bank's WDI indicators of human development. The tax burden and data on outcomes in the international PISA survey regarding school results are from the OECD. The calculations are based on average figures since 2010, except for PISA, which is from the 2022 survey. The outcome in each welfare measure has been calculated so that the country at the top gets a score of 10, the country at the bottom a score of 1, and the others are rated based on the distance to the top and the bottom. Each dimension indicates the average score for the three measures included in the dimension. The total score indicates the average of the four dimensions.

Countries with up to 35 per cent in taxes as a share of GDP (average for the decade) are defined as having a low tax burden; those with between 36 and 40 per cent in taxes as a share of GDP are defined as having a medium tax level; and those with taxes 41 per cent or higher as a share of GDP are defined as having a high tax level.

Research literature supports that higher levels of taxation can affect economic growth negatively, over and beyond certain levels of taxation and government spending (Bergh and Henrekson 2011; Scully 2003). For Australia the optimal growth-inducing level of taxation and government spending has been estimated at 31 per cent tax as a share of GDP level (Makin et al. 2019). This is likely a reference point also for other developed countries. With this benchmark in mind, we believe the tax burden bracket up to 35 per cent of GDP reasonably qualifies as 'low tax' and includes enough countries to allow meaningful comparisons. Countries with a level above this but below 40 per cent can be described as 'medium-tax' nations, while taxes of 41 per cent or higher are typically thought of as characteristic of welfare states. These boundaries were also chosen since the numbers 35 and 40 are round and intuitive, and since this division allows for sorting developed economies with more than one million inhabitants into three large groups based on their tax levels.

The composition of taxes has changed marginally in OECD countries on average over the past decades. Personal income taxes make up a slightly smaller share of the total now compared to the 1970s and 1980s. Instead, general consumption taxes have increased their share. We do not find any link between tax composition and welfare quality or economic growth and therefore do not pursue this issue further.

The results from the four areas of unemployment, health, education and exclusion are combined into an overall rating. Japan receives the highest overall rating in welfare, followed by South Korea and Switzerland. Three low-tax countries thus end up at the top with the best welfare outcomes. This is followed by Norway and Germany, two countries with medium-high taxes. Among the top five countries there is no high-tax country with a tax burden above 40 per cent. High-tax countries Austria and Denmark appear only in 7th and 8th places. Sweden ranks 12th, in the middle of the spread.

The correlation is clear in Figure 1, which shows the relationship between grades in the welfare index's combined measure and the tax burden. Countries with a higher tax burden tend to have worse outcomes in terms of welfare. As will be shown later in this book, this is also seen for three of the welfare areas individually, while the fourth, exclusion, tends to have better outcomes in high-tax countries. Overall, high taxes are clearly not a guarantee of good welfare outcomes.

Figure 1 Combined score for four welfare dimensions, average since 2010

Sources: World Bank's WDI indicators (most welfare data) and OECD (PISA and taxes).

Notes: Relative score on a scale of 1–10 with 10 the best and 1 the worst outcome. Each dimension is the average of three subdimensions. The combined score is the average of four dimensions. Average data since 2010 for each subdimension. Dimension is Unemployment.

A broad comparison of the economically advanced nations with a million or more adult inhabitants shows that on average low-tax countries have managed to deliver better welfare with less tax burden. A common question in the social sciences is whether correlations such as those in Figure 1 can be interpreted as causation. For our purposes, however, this issue is less relevant. We do not want to claim that lower taxes cause better welfare. Rather, the important insight from the data is that it is possible to achieve better outcomes with less tax revenue.

A hypothesis is that governments (or voters) in some countries whose people prefer lower taxes tend to be more concerned with the efficient delivery of welfare. This mechanism is corroborated further in a later chapter on welfare state crowding out. Yet some low-tax countries also have poor outcomes, so low-tax countries are not inherently immune to political and administrative failures that lead to poor welfare quality.

Another statistical question would be whether low-tax countries benefit from better conditions, for example, abundant natural resources, which would allow them to spend a smaller proportion of GDP but still have more money at their disposal. However, it is difficult to claim such a relationship. One might make a case about Norway, rich in oil and gas, having a medium instead of high level of taxation as the oil revenues are so significant. On the whole though, it is not natural resource abundance that is linked with having either high or low tax levels. Several low-tax countries that fare best in the welfare league, such as Japan, South Korea or Switzerland, do not in fact have many natural resources at all.

Another hypothesis might be that countries with a homogeneous population would have an easier time getting good welfare outcomes and a stronger public opinion for higher taxes. However, a number of countries with mixed populations, such as New Zealand, Australia, Canada and Switzerland, have very good welfare outcomes.

Some homogeneous countries such as Japan and South Korea have remarkably low taxes.

The following chapters delve more deeply into the respective welfare categories.

3 LOW-TAX COUNTRIES LEAD AND LAG IN HEALTHCARE

First, a compilation of three current health measures that are included in the comprehensive index – life expectancy, maternal mortality and number of hospital beds per inhabitant – are used in this chapter to compare welfare in terms of health.[1] Then more detailed measures that are not always available for all countries corroborate the overall results and provide insight into how some low-tax countries succeed.

Clearly, the Anglo-Saxon systems of UK, Canada and the US do not lead to the best health outcomes. Yet, low-tax countries such as Switzerland or Japan top the health dimension. The results for the health dimension are summarised in Table 4. Overall, Japan and South Korea, two low-tax countries, that end up at the top in terms of health. Norway, Iceland and Germany are ranked next – three countries with a medium-tax burden. No high-tax country is among the top five countries with the best health. Interestingly,

1 Infant mortality is often compared, but countries use different definitions. Therefore maternal mortality can be a more reliable indicator of quality in prenatal and natal care.

the top as well as the bottom of the list is dominated by low-tax countries. This underlines our conclusion that world-leading welfare *can* be created with low taxes, not that it necessarily does so automatically.

Table 4 Health

		Health (a)	*Life expectancy (b)*	*Maternal mortality (c)*	*Sick beds (d)*	*Taxes (e)*
1	Japan	9.5	83.7	5	13	30 (low)
2	South Korea	7.5	82.0	7	11	26 (low)
3	Norway	6.6	82.3	3	4	40 (medium)
4	Iceland	6.5	82.6	3	3	36 (medium)
5	Germany	6.5	80.8	5	8	38 (medium)
6	Austria	6.4	81.3	6	8	42 (high)
7	Spain	6.4	82.9	4	3	34 (low)
8	Switzerland	6.4	83.2	7	5	27 (low)
9	Australia	6.2	82.5	5	4	27 (low)
10	France	6.1	82.3	8	6	45 (high)
11	Italy	6.0	82.7	6	3	43 (high)
12	Belgium	5.9	81.1	5	6	43 (high)
13	Sweden	5.7	82.3	5	2	43 (high)
14	Netherlands	5.5	81.5	5	4	38 (medium)
15	Greece	5.5	81.1	5	4	38 (medium)
16	Finland	5.2	81.3	7	5	43 (high)
17	Ireland	5.2	81.6	6	3	24 (low)
18	Denmark	4.8	80.7	6	3	46 (high)
19	New Zealand	4.7	81.6	8	3	32 (low)
20	UK	4.3	81.0	9	3	33 (low)
21	Canada	4.1	81.8	12	3	33 (low)
22	Portugal	4.1	80.9	10	3	34 (low)
23	US	1.1	78.3	17	3	25 (low)

(a) Average grade (scale 1–10) for dimension health; (b) life expectancy at birth (years), average since 2010; (c) maternal mortality (per 100,000 births), average since 2010; (d) sick beds per 1,000 inhabitants, average since 2010; (e) taxes as share of GDP (%), average since 2010.

Sources: Data on outcomes in unemployment, health and exclusion are different indicators from the World Bank's WDI indicators of human development. The tax burden is from the OECD. The calculations are based on average figures since 2010, except for PISA, which is from the 2022 survey. The outcome in each welfare measure has been calculated so that the country at the top gets a score of 10, the country at the bottom a score of 1, and the others are rated based on the distance to the top and the bottom. Each dimension indicates the average score for the three measures included in the dimension. The total score indicates the average of the four dimensions.

Figure 2 Life expectancy at birth, average since 2010

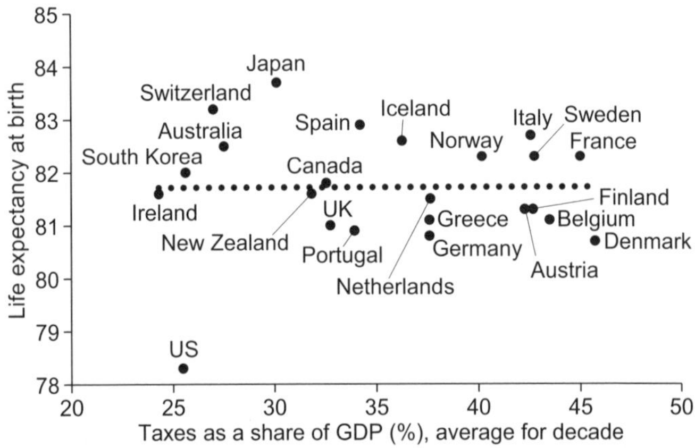

Sources: World Bank's WDI indicators (welfare data) and OECD (taxes).

Figure 2 shows the relationship between life expectancy at birth and the tax burden. There is no systematic relationship here, as the US with a low tax burden has an unusually low life expectancy. If the US were excluded from the analysis, there would be a strong correlation between higher life expectancy and lower tax burden. Figure 3 shows sick beds per thousand inhabitants, where we clearly see that the density of sick beds is actually higher in the countries with a lower tax burden. A high number of sick beds per inhabitant does not necessarily have to be a sign of well-functioning healthcare but still shows that low-tax countries manage to invest sufficient resources and avoid bottlenecks.

Figure 3 Sick beds per 1,000 inhabitants, average since 2010

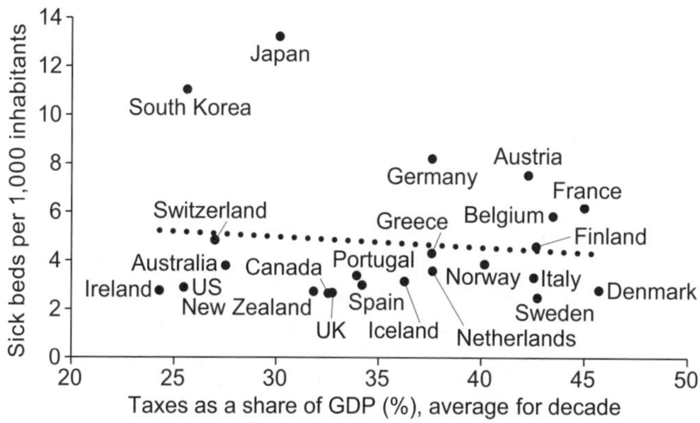

Sources: World Bank's WDI indicators (welfare data) and OECD (taxes).

Figure 4, which shows the extent of maternal mortality, is the only dimension in this comparison in which high-tax countries have better outcomes. High-tax countries have lower levels of maternal mortality. The other two health measures, life expectancy at birth and sick beds per inhabitant, show better outcomes for the low-tax countries. In the dimension of health, on average the low-tax countries perform better, albeit by a narrow margin, and a number of low-tax countries top the league. It is possible that the maternal mortality statistics of the US is somewhat inflated, by the country not following the same classification standards for live births. However, as the methodology of this book is to mainly rely on World Development Indicators data from the World Bank, this international standardised measure is used.

Figure 4 Maternal mortality per 100,000 births, average since 2010

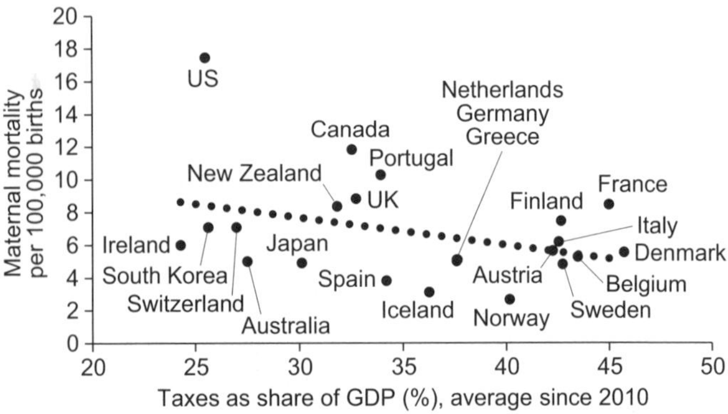

Sources: World Bank's WDI indicators (welfare data) and OECD (taxes).

One conclusion is that some low-tax countries have better success in creating successful health systems than others. Another is that the higher tax burdens of the other countries are not actually buying them better healthcare on average, particularly not compared to low-tax nations such as Japan, South Korea and Switzerland which have top-level health outcomes.

Detailed measures of healthcare quality support the comprehensive results

The quality of healthcare is compared in many different ways by various stakeholders. Every metric and ranking can be questioned. Nevertheless, the overall picture provides a clear indication that high-tax countries are no longer ranking in the absolute top tier but have been nudged down by a group of wealthy low-tax countries.

One frequently referenced ranking is from the Prosperity Institute, which focuses on where patients receive the best healthcare.[2] In this ranking, some wealthy Asian countries such as Singapore, Japan, Taiwan and South Korea are at the top, all with lower tax burdens. Switzerland ranks highest in the Euro Health Consumer Index 2018 (see Bjornberg and Phang 2019). Another often-cited ranking of the best-performing healthcare systems comes from the Commonwealth Fund.[3] Their ranking includes only 11 countries, among which Norway, the Netherlands and Australia are at the top, while Sweden ranks 7th.[4]

Another type of study focuses on five-year survival rates, that is, the survival rate of people diagnosed with

2 https://www.prosperity.com/rankings (the Prosperity Institute was until recently the Legatum Institute).

3 https://www.commonwealthfund.org/publications/fund-reports/2021/aug/mirror-mirror-2021-reflecting-poorly

4 Similar rankings are found in the Health and Access Quality (HAQ) Index that aims to evaluate access to and quality of healthcare in 195 countries. The index is based on the Global Burden of Diseases, Injuries and Risk Factor Study 2016.

cancer five years after treatment. For example, it is sometimes claimed that Sweden has among the highest survival rates following a cancer diagnosis, referencing a review in *The Lancet* (Allemani et al. 2018). Actually, however, the review lists a number of low-tax countries as having the highest survival rates, with Sweden at the top only among included European countries.

To further illustrate how successful low-tax countries compare with high-tax countries, a representative selection from the OECD's statistics collection, *Health at a Glance 2023* (OECD 2023), is presented below.

Table 5 Countries with the highest healthcare share of GDP

US	16.6	UK	11.3	Iceland	8.6
France	12.1	Sweden	10.7	Norway	7.9
Japan	11.5	South Korea	9.7		
Switzerland	11.3	Denmark	9.5		

Source: OECD (2023).

These data are not age adjusted. Such adjustment can sometimes be crucial because countries differ significantly in demographic composition. A country with a disproportionately young, prime-age population will naturally incur lower healthcare costs, as that age group tends to be the healthiest. However, the rich countries compared here, especially the ones at the top of the league in the table do not differ all that much in their age profile.

One measure of health-related welfare is the proportion of people who perceive themselves to be in good health, according to the OECD's health database. In Sweden, 76 per cent consider themselves to be in good or very good health, marginally higher than in the Netherlands (75 per cent) but significantly lower than in low-tax Switzerland (81 per cent) and Ireland (84 per cent).

There does not seem to be a close relationship between the tax burden and the proportion of GDP allocated to healthcare. Table 5 shows the OECD countries with the highest healthcare expenditures. These include both high-tax countries such as France and Sweden and low-tax countries such as Japan and Switzerland, which also perform well in terms of healthcare outcomes. Tables 6–11 present supporting evidence, with data for some of the developed economies of the world. The point is that these data, with different sets of health dimensions being measured, also support the systematic analysis above for 23 advanced economies with an adult population of more than a million. In addition, these tables cast light on how successful countries organise their healthcare.

Table 6 Avoidable deaths per year and 100,000 people

Switzerland	133	Australia	144	France	160
Japan	134	Italy	146	Netherlands	161
Israel	141	Luxembourg	147	Denmark	174
Iceland	142	Sweden	150	UK	222
South Korea	142	Norway	156	US	336

Source: OECD (2023). Calculated with an estimation method based on the WHO mortality database and the Eurostat data on causes of death.

An overarching measure of healthcare quality is considered to be so-called avoidable mortality. This is defined as mortality due to lack of effective healthcare interventions, including medical errors, or due to lack of proper preventive care. This statistic follows an international standard for collating and estimating how many deaths could have been avoided with timely and effective healthcare interventions and effective public health and prevention.[5] Table 6 shows the ranking of avoidable deaths per 100,000 people. Here, six low-tax countries rank at the top. Avoidable deaths are fewest in Switzerland and Japan, while the US and the UK perform poorly.

The picture is more mixed for another common measure, so-called 30-day mortality rate after a heart attack or stroke. But again, several low-tax countries also rank highly, as shown in Table 7.

Table 7 30-day mortality after a hospital episode, percentage of those diagnosed in a hospital

	Cardiac arrest	*Stroke*		*Cardiac arrest*	*Stroke*
Japan	8.3	2.9	Australia	3.3	4.8
Iceland	1.7	3.1	Netherlands	2.9	4.9
Norway	2.6	3.1	Denmark	4.8	4.9
South Korea	8.4	3.3	Israel	5.2	5.4
US	5.5	4.3	Sweden	3.6	5.5

Source: OECD (2023).

The Achilles' heel of some high-tax countries' healthcare has traditionally been considered to be waiting times and lack of accessibility. This is confirmed by the figures reported by the OECD, such as the proportion of the population satisfied with accessibility. In Table 8 a selection of countries is shown to illustrate the range between some of the successful low- and high-tax countries such as

5 For a description of methodology, see https://www.oecd.org/content/dam/oecd/en/data/datasets/oecd-health-statistics/avoidable-mortality-2019-joint-oecd-eurostat-list-preventable-treatable-causes-of-death.pdf.

Sweden and France. But some low-tax countries such as the UK also do poorly.

Mirroring the results in Table 8, high-tax countries such as Sweden and France typically appear to ration the number of visits. Table 9 shows that Swedes relatively rarely get to see a doctor. At the same time, OECD figures indicate that Sweden still has a relatively large number of doctors per capita and that the number of doctors has increased significantly over the past decade. Patients in low-tax South Korea and Japan, in contrast, appear to have easy access to doctors.

Table 8 Share of the population that is satisfied with accessibility of healthcare (selection of countries)

Switzerland	94	US	75
Luxembourg	86	Sweden	74
Netherlands	83	South Korea	74
Norway	80	France	71
Japan	76	UK	67

Source: OECD (2023).

Table 9 Number of meetings with a doctor per inhabitant and year (selection of countries)

South Korea	15.7	Israel	7.2	Denmark	3.8
Japan	11.1	France	5.5	US	3.4
Netherlands	8.6	Norway	3.9	Sweden	2.3

Source: OECD (2023).

In fact, patients in low-tax Switzerland are much more satisfied with the time they have with their doctor during the few occasions they meet, as shown in Table 10.

Table 10 Share of respondents (%) who agree that doctors have enough time with patients (selection of countries)

Israel	97	France	84
Netherlands	94	US	83
Switzerland	86	Sweden	69

Source: OECD (2023).

Healthcare and social care also include other aspects, such as how many people receive old age care in some form. However, even in this regard, there are low-tax countries that perform better than high-tax countries such as Denmark and Sweden, as shown in Table 11.

Table 11 Share above age 65 that receives old age care (selection of countries)

Israel	27.8	Denmark	14.3
Switzerland	24.2	Australia	14.1
Sweden	15.7	Netherlands	11.7
Norway	14.6	US	1.7

Source: OECD (2023).

Overall, this partial but not unrepresentative selection of healthcare quality metrics confirms that several successful low-tax countries often rank at the top, surpassing high-tax countries that are frequently claimed to deliver the best welfare. This also contains lessons for the low-tax countries like the UK that perform poorly in healthcare.[6]

6 Niemietz (2024) provides a blueprint of how the UK could replace the NHS with an insurance system more like those in the Netherlands or Switzerland.

So, how do some low-tax countries like Switzerland and Japan consistently rank at the top? The next section provides examples of how these countries succeed without compromising universal access to high-quality care.

Lessons from healthcare organisation in Switzerland and Japan

The Swiss healthcare system is based on private insurance that has been mandatory since 1996 and achieves universal coverage.[7] Since then, all residents of Switzerland must purchase individual private health insurance. Public, non-profit and for-profit providers deliver healthcare services.

Choice of co-payment scheme reduces excessive demand without hurting low-income patients

Insurance companies are not allowed to deny individuals access to standard insurance plans, although they may decline optional supplementary insurance. While insurers must not make a profit on standard insurance, they are allowed to profit on supplemental plans. Insurance fees are effectively linked to income (up to a point), because public funding is provided for those who cannot afford insurance. There are also means-tested exemptions from co-payments. Overall, low-income individuals

7 The following description is partly based on Forum för Health Policy (2017) and Lundbäck (2022).

typically pay less for healthcare than high-income earners. Also, citizens can choose higher co-payments in return for lower insurance fees. For those who can afford it, co-payments can range from approximately 300 CHF to 2,500 CHF. Empirical research has long shown that higher co-payments reduce overutilisation of care.

Because co-payments are optional and typically chosen by higher-income individuals, low-income patients are not discouraged from seeking care. Consequently, Switzerland scores highly on equity in access to care, as noted in earlier Commonwealth Fund rankings.

As a result of optional co-payments, approximately one-quarter of Swiss healthcare is financed through out-of-pocket payments, compared to 14 per cent in Sweden. Nonetheless, the percentage of GDP spent on healthcare in Switzerland (including co-payments) is not vastly different from that in Sweden. This means that Switzerland saves public funds and can maintain lower taxes.

Insurers with many low-risk members contribute to a redistribution fund that subsidises insurers with high-risk members. Since 2012, age, sex and prior hospitalisations have been included as factors in this redistribution. At the same time, Switzerland adopted a case-based payment system (Diagnosis-Related Groups (DRGs)) and implemented mechanisms to ensure care quality. For example, the National Association for Quality Improvement in Hospitals and Clinics (ANQ) conducts ongoing quality measurements.

The extensive choice available to individuals not only allows them to select their healthcare provider but also to decide how they want their care organised, creating strong incentives for innovation. By choosing a contract-based care model, such as a Health Maintenance Organisation (HMO), a family doctor model or a telemedicine model, patients limit their freedom of choice but benefit from lower premiums or other favourable terms. Integrated care models like HMOs, where primary care doctors are employed by the organisation, are becoming increasingly common. Telemedicine models, in which patients initially contact a call centre for guidance, are other newer options.

Over time, the proportion of Swiss citizens choosing alternative care models that limit personal choice has grown significantly. Contract-based care tends to improve efficiency, partly because it fosters effective care pathways compared to a fully open system where patients freely shop around (see, for example, Kreier and Zweifel 2010).

More Swiss than Swedes receive old age care

More Swiss residents than Swedes receive old age care. About two-thirds of providers are public or non-profit, while one-third are for-profit. Elderly care facilities, including nursing and retirement homes, can be public, non-profit or for-profit. For-profit facilities generally do not receive direct public subsidies. Non-profit facilities require residents to cover housing costs if they can afford them; otherwise, subsidies are provided.

Switzerland does not have a fee ceiling as many countries do that effectively subsidise higher-income individuals. This policy, along with higher co-payments in healthcare, is one reason why Switzerland can invest more in healthcare and old age care while spending less taxpayer money. Additionally, institutional competition among insurers, healthcare organisations and payment models drives continual efficiency improvements, resulting in shorter wait times and better outcomes.

Several analyses, summarised by Sanandaji and Sahlgren (2019a), indicate that Switzerland, in some respects, provides more equitable access to care than a high-tax country like Sweden. Absolute inequality in mortality by education level among men is roughly the same in both countries. For women, mortality inequality is significantly lower in Switzerland. Among the lowest-income fifth of the population, 66.6 per cent in Switzerland report good health, slightly higher than the 63.6 per cent in the same group in Sweden. Among the highest-income fifth, 86.1 per cent in Sweden and 85.9 per cent in Switzerland report good health. By this measure, class disparities are greater in Sweden than in Switzerland. A possible explanation is that rationing and queues are more prevalent in Sweden.

Japanese healthcare. Japan's health insurance system provides universal coverage, primarily funded through taxes, individual premiums and a 30 per cent co-payment with caps for high medical costs. Young children and low-income elderly individuals benefit from lower co-payment levels, and there is an annual maximum household co-payment based on age and income. Over 70 per cent of the population also opts for secondary, voluntary private insurance, covering areas like dental care or additional income during illness. Out-of-pocket spending accounts for 14 per cent of healthcare costs, approximately the same as in Sweden.

Private medical schools help avoid doctor shortages

An intriguing feature of Japan's healthcare system is that approximately one-third of medical students study at private medical schools, paying higher tuition fees. This has allowed Japan to avoid the recruitment issues faced by many countries like the Nordics, which depend significantly on attracting doctors from abroad.

Historically, there has been no institutional or financial distinction between primary and specialised care in Japan. The concept of 'general practice' has only recently developed. Primary care is primarily provided at clinics, with some services offered in the outpatient departments of hospitals. Most clinics (83 per cent as of 2015) are privately owned and operated by physicians or healthcare companies (typically controlled by doctors). A smaller proportion is owned by local governments, public agencies or non-profit organisations.

Patients are not required to register with a particular clinic, and there is no strict 'gatekeeping'. However, the government encourages patients to select their doctors, and additional fees apply for initial consultations at large hospitals. Acute care hospitals – both public and private

– can choose to be reimbursed either strictly per service (following the national fee schedule) or through the Diagnosis Procedure Combination (DPC) system, a case-based classification similar to DRGs. Most acute care hospitals opt for the DPC method. The national fee schedule is revised every two years by the government following negotiations with stakeholders.

The widespread adoption of an advanced DRG-like reimbursement system in Japan creates strong incentives for efficiency.

In sum, Switzerland and Japan differ in many respects but share critical similarities, which contribute to their success in healthcare outcomes:

- Diversity in healthcare provision: both countries have a mix of public, private and non-profit healthcare providers. Japan has private medical schools, while Switzerland emphasises patient choice among providers.
- Mandatory insurance with redistribution: both systems rely on mandatory health insurance, with publicly governed redistribution mechanisms and regulated premiums.
- Efficiency mechanisms: in Switzerland, competition among insurers drives the development of integrated or contract-based care solutions. In Japan, the DRG-like reimbursement system incentivises efficiency across the healthcare sector.

4 COUNTRIES WITH LOWER TAXES OFFER BETTER EDUCATION

A common motive for high taxes is to be able to finance good education for everyone. However, the international comparisons clearly show that low-tax economies have better education results.[1]

The results of the international comparisons are shown in Table 12. For the dimension of education in our welfare index, it is very clear that the low-tax countries succeed best with welfare. At the top are Japan and South Korea, two low-tax countries that generally have good welfare outcomes. Canada, Ireland and Australia also rank among the top. They are followed by Switzerland and New Zealand. The seven countries that succeed best in the international PISA tests all have lower tax burdens.

Figures 5–7 show the results of the latest global PISA test conducted in 2022, which measures 15-year-olds' knowledge and skills in mathematics (Figure 5), science

1 There is a discussion of measurement issues in PISA that could affect cross-national comparison. However, there is no particular reason to assume that such measurement issues would be systematically linked to countries' tax burden. If the limitations are randomly scattered across countries, then the results are unaffected.

(Figure 6) and reading comprehension (Figure 7) respectively. In all three subjects low-tax countries perform better.

Table 12 Education

		Education (a)	*Mathematics (b)*	*Reading (c)*	*Science (d)*	*Tax burden (e)*
1	Japan	10	536	516	547	30 (low)
2	South Korea	9.2	527	515	528	26 (low)
3	Canada	7.7	497	507	515	33 (low)
4	Ireland	7.5	492	516	504	24 (low)
5	Australia	6.8	487	498	507	27 (low)
6	Switzerland	6.7	508	483	503	27 (low)
7	New Zealand	6.6	479	501	504	32 (low)
8	Finland	6.6	484	490	511	43 (high)
9	UK	6.5	489	494	500	33 (low)
10	US	6.2	465	504	499	25 (low)
11	Denmark	6.2	489	489	494	46 (high)
12	Sweden	5.9	482	487	494	43 (high)
13	Austria	5.7	487	480	491	42 (high)
14	Belgium	5.7	489	479	491	43 (high)
15	Germany	5.4	475	480	492	38 (high)
16	Netherlands	5	493	459	488	38 (medium)
17	France	5	474	474	487	45 (high)
18	Portugal	4.9	472	477	484	34 (low)
19	Italy	4.9	471	482	477	43 (high)
20	Spain	4.9	473	474	485	34 (low)
21	Norway	4.7	468	477	478	40 (mediun)
22	Iceland	2	459	436	447	36 (medium)
23	Greece	1.1	430	438	441	38 (medium)

(a) Average grade (scale 1–10) for dimension education; (b)–(d) PISA 2022 results; (e) taxes as share of GDP (%), average since 2010.

Sources: The tax burden and data on outcomes in the international PISA survey regarding school results are from the OECD. Data are from the latest 2022 PISA survey.

Figure 5 Average PISA 2022 results: mathematics

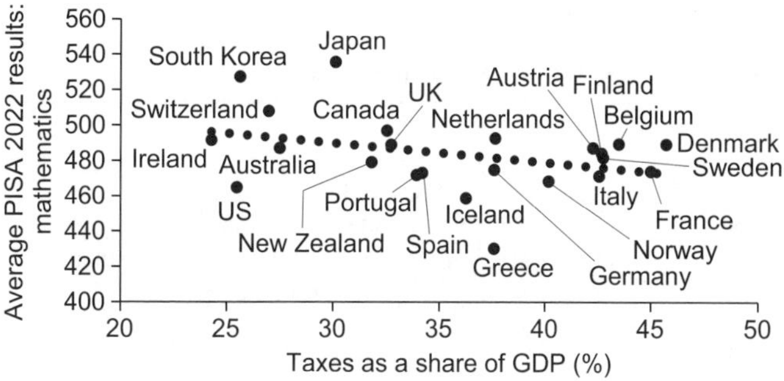

Sources: OECD (PISA and taxes).

Estonia is not part of this study, since the country has just shy of a million adult inhabitants, which was a criterion set for inclusion in the dataset. Yet the country is a prime example of how good school results in reading, science and mathematics can be achieved in a system with low taxes. The schools are mainly publicly funded and run, but 11 per cent of pupils attend private primary schools. Parents and students choose a school, and admission is often based on grades. Private schools have the right to supplement their budget with fees from parents. All schools have a great deal of autonomy. Schools can hire the teachers they want, determine the teachers' salaries and offer special profile subjects. Schools also have the right to group by level when they think that is effective. School bureaucracy is kept limited, partly made more efficient by digitisation. Both primary and secondary school ends with a national exam. Efficient schools that foster grit and imprint knowledge are not necessarily those that have the most funds; it is more about creating a good teacher-led model.

Figure 6 Average PISA 2022 results: science

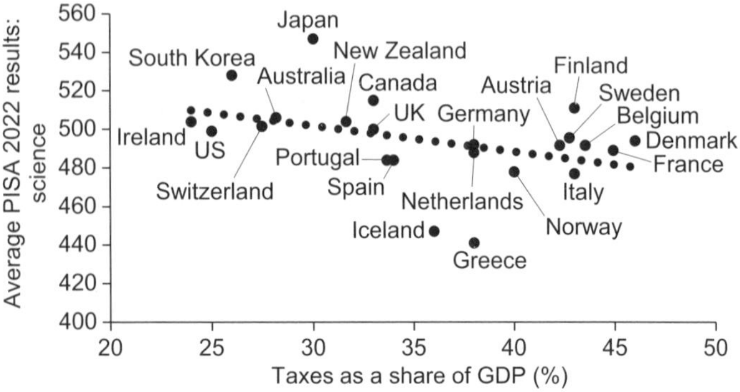

Sources: OECD (PISA and taxes).

Ireland with its small government is another European country that thrives in its educational outcomes, with public funding of schools and a mix of private and public schools. The Irish education system is based on the state paying for education in schools that typically are owned and operated by non-state actors.

A systematic review of the research literature on school reforms over the past decades is found in Blix and Jordahl (2021). Although it is not entirely easy to determine why educational outcomes have declined in high-tax countries, it appears to be well-established that the causes are neither a lack of resources, the slowly increasing proportion of private providers of education nor the fact that some of these are profit driven.

Figure 7 Average PISA 2022 results: reading

Sources: OECD (PISA and taxes).

Instead, the causes seem to be pedagogical trends, the introduction of inconsistent curricula, a higher proportion of recently immigrated students and, not least, teachers' increasingly limited ability to maintain order in the classroom. One of the world's leading education researchers, Eric A. Hanushek, has been a sharp critic of how public funds are spent on education and the return on that investment (see, for example, Hanushek 1994). His work is often cited to challenge advocates of public schooling who call for increased resources. However, Hanushek argues that while more funding could indeed improve student outcomes, this cannot be achieved merely by adding money and expecting good results.[2] Success requires the

2 See, for example, https://hanushek.stanford.edu/opinions/does-money-matter-after-all.

proper use of resources, and an education system organised in line with what research has shown.

Overall, the education sector shows the same pattern as other welfare areas. High-tax countries have fallen behind, while several low-tax countries are claiming top positions. One possible interpretation of this pattern is that incentives play a role. In high-tax countries it is less worthwhile to strive for better-paying jobs. As a result, parents and pupils may perceive that grit and knowledge are not important, and neither is demanding that schools focus on knowledge and achievement.

Ireland and Estonia versus Sweden is a good example. Sweden was long famous for its well-functioning educational model and established itself as one of Europe's leading knowledge economies. Ireland and Estonia were both behind, but have caught up through low taxes and business-friendly policies. As many tech companies are attracted from abroad and growing through local entrepreneurship, this also leads to a greater focus on education. Possible mechanisms include foreign experts and their families migrating and increasing the demand for higher quality schools, that students and parents are aware of the rising future opportunities being created and the low taxes meaning that incentives are strong, and that local communities as a whole treasure knowledge more when the nation is growing strong as a knowledge economy.

In countries such as Sweden, where the level of development is good but economic growth is stagnating under high taxes and incentives for the individual are limited, pupils, parents, teachers and overall society are less focused on hard work in school being the path to the future. Similar encouragement exists, but not on the same level, as human behaviour adapts to the incentive structures of society. Norms of hard work in school ultimately are linked to taxation of future incomes, through the expectations of pupils, parents and teachers.

5 HIGH-TAX NATIONS TEND TO HAVE HIGHER UNEMPLOYMENT RATES EVEN FOR LOW-INCOME GROUPS

The dimension of unemployment consists of the three submeasures of unemployment for those with basic, intermediate and advanced degrees. As shown in Table 13, South Korea and Japan, two low-tax countries, have the lowest unemployment rates. This is followed by Norway, Iceland and Germany, which are economies with a medium tax burden. No high-tax country is among the top five countries.

A substantial research literature shows that lower taxes on work or lower contributions causally increase incentives to participate in the workforce (see the literature review in Lundberg and Norell (2020)). Married women, single mothers and wage earners close to retirement appear to be particularly sensitive to such incentives. To some extent, of course, the effect of higher taxes on work can be counteracted by other elements such as a family policy that makes it easy and profitable for parents of young children to work, a higher general retirement age or effective labour market training and programmes.

Table 13 Unemployment

		(a)	*(b)*	*(c)*	*(d)*	*Taxes (e)*
1	South Korea	9.7	2.7	3.3	3.7	26 (low)
2	Japan	9.6		4.0	2.8	30 (low)
3	Norway	9.3	8.2	3.3	2.3	40 (medium)
4	Iceland	9.1	7.5	4.3	3.0	36 (medium)
5	Germany	8.9	10.3	4.1	2.3	38 (medium)
6	Switzerland	8.8	8.5	4.6	3.3	27 (low)
7	Netherlands	8.8	8.4	5.0	3.2	38 (medium)
8	New Zealand	8.7	7.7	5.8	3.3	32 (low)
9	Australia	8.4	10.4	5.6	3.2	27 (low)
10	Austria	8.4	11.5	4.8	3.3	42 (high)
11	UK	8.3	10.4	6.5	3.3	33 (low)
12	Denmark	8.2	10.2	5.4	4.5	46 (high)
13	US	8.1	9.2	8.0	3.7	25 (low)
14	Belgium	7.6	13.7	7.2	4.0	43 (high)
15	Canada	7.0	14.1	8.5	5.4	33 (low)
16	Sweden	6.9	20.1	6.3	4.2	43 (high)
17	Finland	6.8	16.7	8.6	4.6	43 (high)
18	Italy	6.7	13.7	9.8	6.1	43 (high)
19	France	6.6	15.8	9.5	5.6	45 (high)
20	Portugal	6.4	10.9	11.5	7.7	34 (low)
21	Ireland	6.3	15.4	11.6	5.5	24 (low)
22	Spain	2.4	26.3	19.1	11.4	34 (low)
23	Greece	1.6	21.8	22.5	15.1	38 (medium)

(a) Average grade (scale 1–10) for dimension unemployment. Unemployment among those with (b) basic, (c) intermediate and (d) advanced education (%), average since 2010. (e) Taxes as share of GDP (%), average since 2010.

Sources: Unemployment data from the World Bank's WDI indicators of human development. Data for unemployment among those with basic education are missing for Japan. The score of the country is based on the other two measures.

Precisely these elements also make it more difficult to interpret comparisons of the employment rate rather than the unemployment rate between countries.

Employment statistics often compare people who work at least one hour a week, which may be part-time work or part of a labour market programme. How many people want to work is affected by such programmes, but also by culture and attitudes that are not necessarily expressions of better or worse welfare. Unemployment is more readily interpreted because it captures how many people want a job but are unable to get one. Therefore, the focus here is on unemployment and its distribution by educational levels. Table 13 shows the ranking of countries.

Figure 8 Unemployment among those with basic education, average since 2010

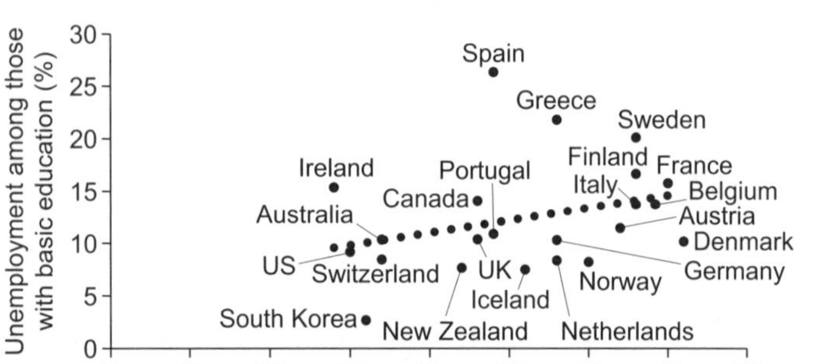

Sources: World Bank's WDI indicators (welfare data) and OECD (taxes).

As can be seen in Figure 8, there is a strong relationship for those with a low level of education, where countries with a high tax burden also have significantly higher unemployment. Even for those with medium (Figure 9) and high (Figure 10) levels of education there is a similar relationship, where unemployment tends to be higher in the countries with a higher tax burden, but the relationship is significantly stronger for the less educated. The level of unemployment, especially among the less educated, is systematically higher among countries with a higher tax rate. This indicates that generous welfare systems create a poverty trap, characterised by dependency on benefits and high thresholds into the labour market.

Figure 9 Unemployment among those with intermediate education, average since 2010

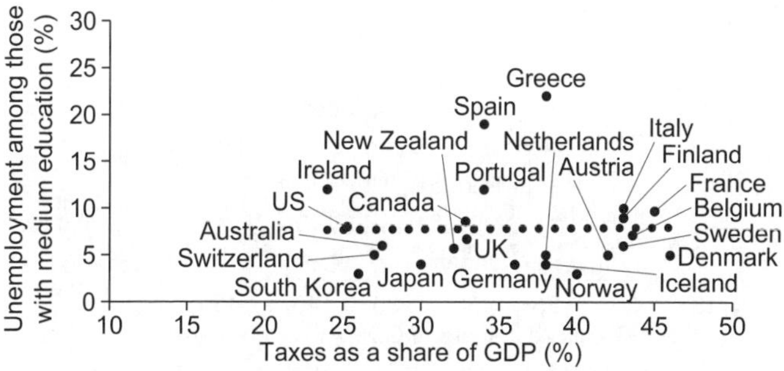

Sources: World Bank's WDI indicators (welfare data) and OECD (taxes).

What drives the connection between taxes and unemployment? Tax on work is a wedge between the value produced and how much the employee receives in wages. If there is an agreed or statutory minimum wage, according to the economic research in the field, it can easily happen that workers with low productivity are not employable (see, for example, the literature review in OECD (2011)). This effect can be greater than the countervailing one, that higher tax revenues provide room for adjustment measures and training in the event of unemployment. In addition, high taxes and the high benefits can give rise to a poverty trap, where individuals get stuck on benefits because they lose out if they start to work. In particular, single parents with young children may find themselves in a situation where the transition from benefits to work does not increase their income at all.

Figure 10 Unemployment among those with higher education, average since 2010

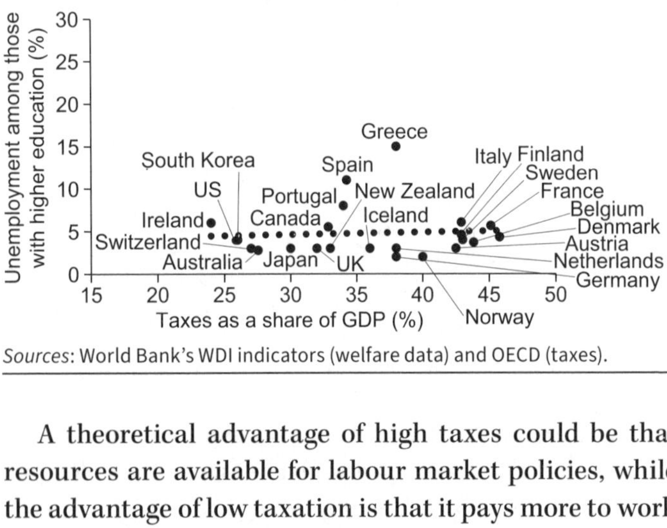

Sources: World Bank's WDI indicators (welfare data) and OECD (taxes).

A theoretical advantage of high taxes could be that resources are available for labour market policies, while the advantage of low taxation is that it pays more to work. Overall, low-tax policies help create a sustainable labour market with low unemployment. Low unemployment among people with low education is also essential to avoid exclusion and inequality.

6 HIGH-TAX NATIONS SUFFER LESS EXCLUSION

Exclusion is the last area studied in our comprehensive index of welfare outcomes (see Table 14). Three central measures of exclusion have been collected from the World Bank's Human Development Indicators: the share of people of working age that are in vulnerable employment; the share living in material poverty (a purchasing power adjusted measure); and the share of young people who neither work nor study, known in the UK as NEETs (Not in Employment, Education or Training).

Norway and Germany, with medium taxes, have overall least exclusion, followed by Denmark, with high taxes, in third place. The low-tax country of Japan comes in fourth place, followed by Iceland with medium-high taxes.

Figure 11 shows the proportion who have vulnerable employment, while Figure 12 shows the proportion of NEETs. Vulnerable employment appears to be slightly lower in countries with higher taxes. However, low-tax US has the lowest percentage of employees with vulnerable employment, while the percentage is highest in South Korea, which also has low taxes.

Table 14 Exclusion

		(a)	(b)	(c)	(d)	(e)
1	Norway	9.1	5.0	0.5	5	40 (medium)
2	Germany	8.8	6.0	0.3	7	38 (medium)
3	Denmark	8.8	5.3	0.4	7	46 (high)
4	Japan	8.6	8.7	1.0	4	30 (low)
5	Iceland	8.5	9.7	0.3	5	36 (medium)
6	Sweden	8.3	6.6	1.1	7	43 (high)
7	Netherlands	8.3	12.4	0.3	5	38 (medium)
8	Finland	8.0	9.7	0.2	9	43 (high)
9	Switzerland	8.0	10.4	0.1	9	27 (low)
10	France	7.6	7.4	0.3	13	45 (high)
11	New Zealand	7.6	16.6		1	32 (low)
12	Belgium	7.6	10.5	0.4	11	43 (high)
13	Australia	7.5	8.8	1.0	10	27 (low)
14	Austria	7.4	9.1	0.9	11	42 (high)
15	US	7.2	4.4	1.8	13	25 (low)
16	UK	6.9	12.7	0.7	12	33 (low)
17	Canada	6.9	10.7	0.8	13	33 (low)
18	Ireland	6.6	11.4	0.9	14	24 (low)
19	South Korea	5.6	20.3	1.7		26 (low)
20	Portugal	5.4	14.1	3.4	11	34 (low)
21	Spain	5.2	11.7	3.1	15	34 (low)
22	Italy	3.7	17.5	3.0	20	43 (high)
23	Greece	1.5	27.1	5.6	17	38 (medium)

(a) Average grade (scale 1–10) for dimension exclusion; (b) share in vulnerable employment (%), average since 2010; (c) share in material poverty (less than 6.85 USD 2017 per day, PPP, %), average since 2010; (d) share of NEETs in the young population (%), average since 2010; (e) taxes as share of GDP (%), average since 2010.

Sources: Exclusion data from the World Bank's WDI indicators of human development. Data on share in material poverty for New Zealand are missing. Data on the share of youth neither in education, employment nor training in South Korea are also missing. The scores of the countries are based on the two existing measures.

Figure 11 Share in vulnerable employment, average since 2010

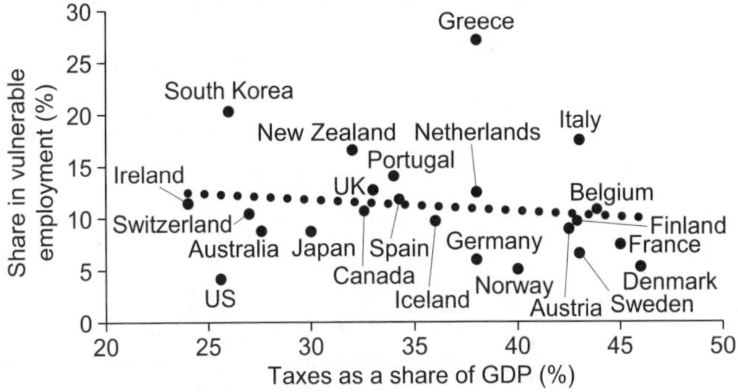

Sources: World Bank's WDI indicators (welfare data) and OECD (taxes).

Figure 12 Share in passive youth, average since 2010

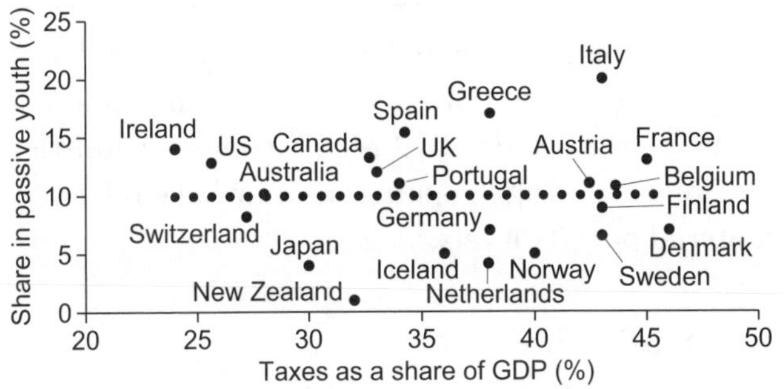

Sources: World Bank's WDI indicators (welfare data) and OECD (taxes).

The proportion of inactive young people has no clear connection with the tax burden (Figure 12). The proportion of young people who are inactive in the high-tax countries is roughly the same as in the low-tax countries. It is reasonable to think that high-tax systems both activate passive young people through labour market programmes but also 'passivise' them through subsidies and high tax thresholds.

Figure 13 Share in material poverty, average since 2010

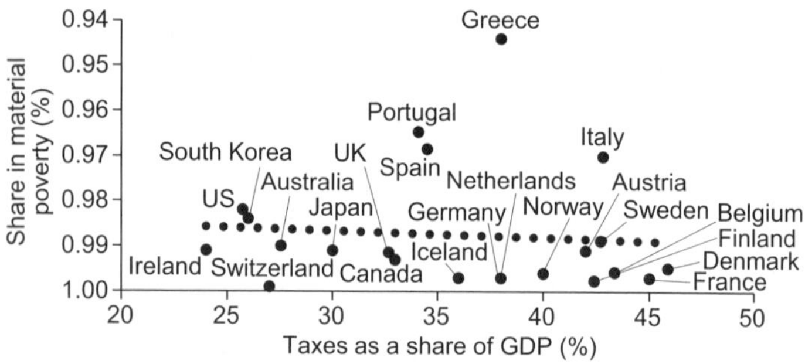

Sources: World Bank's WDI indicators (welfare data) and OECD (taxes).

The proportion living in material poverty is also lower on average in countries with high taxes, as shown in Figure 13. The pattern is also that Mediterranean countries such as Greece, Portugal, Spain and Italy have relatively high material poverty levels.

Income equality

Equality is often regarded as a central aspect of a welfare society. Yet in recent years research has pointed to serious measurement issues and interpretational problems that befall statistics on income inequality, as explained below. Therefore, the comparison in this book does not directly include income equality other than the measure of material poverty above.

A common assumption has been that a market economy and lower taxes automatically lead to greater inequality as less is spent on redistribution. Yet this connection is now being questioned in various strands of recent research.

Some studies examine how economic freedom affects different income groups. Economic freedom is measured using an index that includes tax burden, rule of law, size of the public sector and market openness. Earlier studies produced mixed results, often based on correlations. The latest, more comprehensive studies with extensive data find that all income groups benefit roughly equally from increased economic freedom.[1] This effect remains consistent across the three components of economic freedom: institutional quality, policy quality and a smaller public sector. Increased economic freedom, such as lower taxes, raises incomes for all groups equally.

Broader welfare indices, such as the Social Progress Index (SPI), also show a strong correlation with the economic freedom index. The SPI includes 54 indicators for meeting people's basic social and environmental needs, such as health, housing, sanitation, equality, integration, sustainability and safety.[2]

Recent research has also highlighted increasing challenges with comparing equality between countries and

1 For example, Bergh and Bjørnskov (2021) find that all income groups gain equally from greater economic freedom.

2 The SPI is designed following ideas developed by Nobel prize winners Amartya Sen and Joseph Stiglitz (https://www.socialprogress.org/index/global/results).

over time (see, for example, Finanspolitiska Rådet 2024). For example, an increasing share of young people pursue higher education. During their studies, they have low incomes, but most earn significantly more later in life. In statistics, this appears as increased income inequality when measured annually. But is this really a sign of greater income inequality?

Another statistical issue arises from the sharp increase in housing prices in many countries. When someone sells a home, large capital gains are recorded for that year. However, the seller cannot necessarily afford a larger home with the proceeds. In most countries' statistics, this is registered as a significant increase in income inequality (Roine and Waldenström 2011). But it is debatable whether inequality has really increased.

Immigration and waves of refugees also increase income inequality statistically, even though immigrants have often experienced significant income gains compared to what they earned in their homelands. How should this be interpreted? Similarly, if wealth and inheritance taxes encourage the wealthiest to emigrate, has that really increased inequality?

The statistical distribution of wealth and income is therefore an opaque measure. For that reason, income equality is not included in the comparison in this book. Instead, the focus is how welfare is impacted if, for example, low-income earners lack access to quality education or healthcare; or if labour markets exhibit high unemployment levels for those with lower education levels.

Free economic systems tend to create prosperity, not just for the rich and middle class but also for those with lower incomes. A study of income mobility in Canadian provinces between 1982 and 2018 shows that higher levels of economic freedom are associated with greater absolute income gains for the bottom decile of the income distribution. Higher levels of economic freedom also meant greater economic mobility. In fact, the positive effects of economic freedom were found to be higher for the bottom decile of income earners than for the overall population (Dean and Geloso 2022).

Taxation and government spending can be used to help the less well-off, but it also limits economic progress for all, which also has an effect on those on low incomes. From an ideological perspective, one can argue for taxing the rich and distributing to those on low incomes, but the economy does not function like that. Public welfare systems can be used to alleviate and prevent poverty, but it is not a case of more taxation and government spending always being the answer. Economic freedom that allows for growth is as relevant for the bottom income earners as for others, if not more so since new economic opportunities on the margin are more relevant for those who have a less stable foothold in the labour market.

7 LOWER-TAX COUNTRIES PROSPER MORE

Historically, welfare spending has mainly consisted of wage costs. GDP growth therefore had less significance for the ability to finance welfare because wages increase in step with GDP. Gradually, however, this relationship has changed. The purchase of medicines, medical technology and even treatments from other countries has increased. Imported digital technology plays a greater role for many welfare operations. In addition, other publicly financed sectors such as defence rely more on the purchase of imported technology. As a result, countries with better economic growth can afford better equipment for their welfare sectors.

In each of the five decades following 1970, there is a clear correlation between lower taxes as a share of total economic production and higher economic growth. Figures 14–18 show the relationship between economic growth and the tax burden over the past five decades. In each decade during the 1970s, 1980s, 1990s, 2000s and 2010s, there is a correlation that the countries with lower taxes as a share of total economic production tend to experience the strongest economic growth. The trend for high-tax countries to stagnate economically is present in all of the last five decades.

Figure 14 Prosperity (GDP/capita) growth, average during 1970s

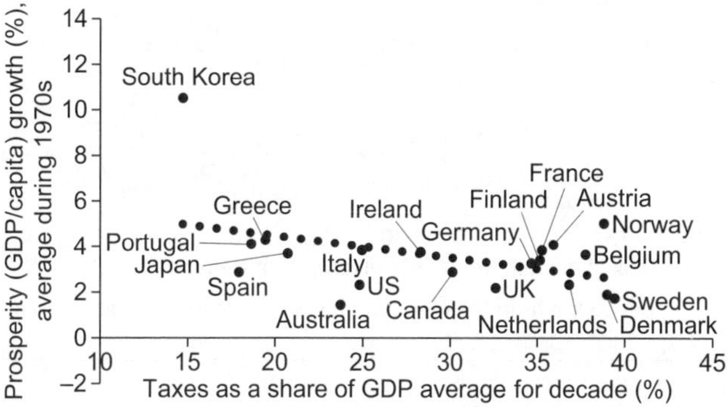

Sources: GDP per capita from the World Bank's WDI indicators; taxes from the OECD.

Figure 15 Prosperity (GDP/capita) growth, average during 1980s

Sources: GDP per capita from the World Bank's WDI indicators; taxes from the OECD.

Figure 16 Prosperity (GDP/capita) growth, average during 1990s

Sources: GDP per capita from the World Bank's WDI indicators; taxes from the OECD.

Figure 17 Prosperity (GDP/capita) growth, average during 2000s

Sources: GDP per capita from the World Bank's WDI indicators; taxes from the OECD.

One might suspect that high taxes are not in themselves the culprit behind the entire shortfall in growth. It could be that countries that choose higher taxes to a certain extent also are prone to other growth-inhibiting policies. However, the research literature provides clear support for causality between taxes as such and economic growth. Most studies find an increase in the size of the public sector by 10 percentage points of GDP causes a lower growth rate in the range of 0.5–1 percentage points per year.[1]

Figure 18 Prosperity (GDP/capita) growth, average during 2010s

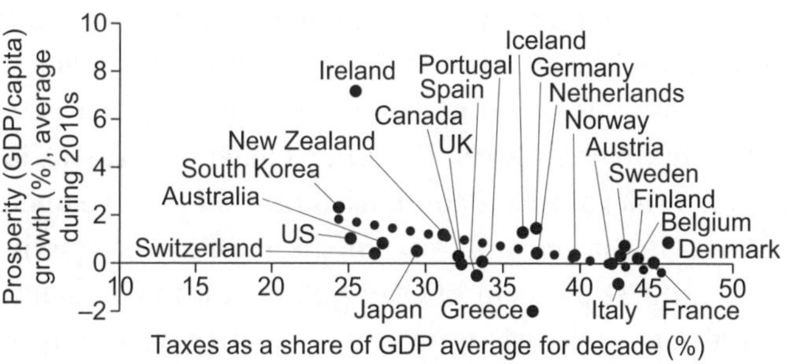

Sources: GDP per capita from the World Bank's WDI indicators; taxes from the OECD.

For example, economists António Afonso and João Tovar Jalles find that public spending has a negative effect on economic growth in OECD countries, mainly due to the negative effects of the resulting higher income taxes. This burden will of course be particularly high if expenditure is wasteful rather than growth-enhancing. Countries experience weaker growth if they have high public sector wage costs, extensive government consumption,

1 A review of studies is provided by Bergh and Henrekson (2016).

extensive government subsidies, and high government debt that entails high interest payments. In contrast, public spending on education and health is positively linked to growth (Afonso and Jalles 2014). Countries with a large public sector thus have lower growth than countries with a small public sector, while it also matters how public funds are spent.

One interesting study by Anthony Makin, Julian Pearce and Shyama Ratnasiri examines the optimal size of the public sector to maximise growth in Australia. The study finds that for the maximum level of economic development, the level of spending should be held to 31 per cent of GDP (Makin et al. 2019). The study focuses on Australia, but is also relevant as a comparison for other developed countries. If the optimal size of the public sector is indeed around 31 per cent of GDP taxation, it makes sense that high-tax nations stagnate in prosperity, as well as in terms of welfare outcome.

8 HIGH-TAX COUNTRIES TREAT SOCIAL PROBLEMS INSTEAD OF PREVENTING THEM

In the US, for many years there has been intense debate over the claim that well-meaning local governments have raised taxes to address social problems but have instead ended up perpetuating poverty and increasing homelessness and crime. There has been much research into the thesis that social spending incentivises social problems instead of addressing the root causes. In his study of San Francisco, for example, Michael Schellenberger (2021) provides much of the statistics and research references, making the case that cities such as San Francisco have exacerbated homelessness with rent controls, building restrictions as well as lax policies towards crime, drugs and public order offences.

Unfortunately, very little research has been done using international comparisons. This chapter is therefore more anecdotal than the previous chapters. Still, important observations can be made, for example, on the failure of high-tax welfare states such as Sweden and France to prevent the emergence of high-crime neighbourhoods. This chapter describes some of these observations heuristically without claiming to have established causal relationships.

The central hypothesis of our theory of 'welfare state crowding out' is that countries more inclined to raise taxes have focused on treating symptoms of social challenges but dodged hard choices that more effectively would have prevented them. Voters who support higher taxes and more generous welfare may be less concerned about whether the design of the welfare system drives up future costs. Eventually, this raises costs or forces cutbacks in welfare in other areas. Where the population more strongly opposes tax increases, governments may feel compelled to plan welfare within tighter budget constraints. Prevention would then appear more urgent.

A metric that captures several aspects of social problems left unaddressed is the mortality rate among young men aged 20–30. This captures shootings, drug overdoses, suicides and traffic fatalities, which in turn represent the tip of the iceberg of social problems that partly emerge in vulnerable areas where many challenged individuals are concentrated.

Table 15 illustrates this with the mortality rate among 25-year-old men in 1970 and in 2021, the latest figures available from the UN mortality database. As seen, the US consistently ranks high in a league of its own in spite of low taxes. There, a decline in murder rates has been offset by the opioid crisis and persistently high traffic fatalities.

Across European countries, there has been a substantial reduction in young men's mortality rates, largely due to improved traffic safety. However, high-tax countries such as Sweden and France have not kept pace and now have the highest mortality rates among young men in the EU. Low-tax countries such as Japan and Singapore, as well as medium-tax Iceland, have achieved the most significant reductions in mortality. Low-tax Switzerland and medium-tax Norway rank in the middle. Apparently, it is possible to address social problems in time even with a low tax rate.

Table 15 Mortality among 25-year old men, annually and per 1,000 inhabitants (selection of countries)

	1970	*2021*
US	2.1	2.0
Sweden	1.3	0.8
Switzerland	1.6	0.5
Netherlands	0.9	0.4
Germany	1.3	0.4
Japan	1.3	0.3
Iceland	1.6	0.3
Singapore	1.6	0.3
Norway	1.3	0.5
France	1.6	0.7
UK	0.9	0.6

Source: UN Human Mortality Database (2023).

Several high-tax countries that once led the welfare rankings have allowed various social challenges to spiral out of control. In high-tax nations such as Sweden or France, for example, less attention has been paid to the efficiency of police and judicial systems or to preventing the emergence of vulnerable areas. Banlieues in France have been an issue for decades while the wave of shootings emanating from Swedish 'miljonprogramsområden' is a more recent phenomenon.

A key question is whether the social costs associated with the growth of vulnerable areas could have been avoided. One explanation involves countries that, earlier than Sweden, either limited immigration or adopted different methods of selecting immigrants. However, this explanation is complicated by the fact that social problems are not primarily caused by recent immigrants themselves. Instead, according to relatively recent and robust research, the costs are exponentially increased by housing policies, urban planning and social policies that lead to the concentration of families facing challenges in certain areas.

For a long time, the evidence was weak that a neighbourhood's socioeconomic composition significantly impacts individual outcomes. This was mainly due to empirical difficulties in proving causation and the lack of differentiation between younger children, older children and teenagers in studies. However, in recent years, several highly credible international studies have provided strong evidence that insufficient attention to social problems in residential environments substantially disadvantages children growing up there in terms of their ability to achieve self-sufficiency as adults.

A researcher's ideal scenario would involve access to data on children randomly distributed across entirely different neighbourhoods and living environments, allowing for a precise assessment of how much the surroundings affect their development. This ideal scenario has actually been realised in the US. The conclusions from this experiment should serve as a wake-up call for several high-tax countries such as France and Sweden as well.[1]

In the early 1990s, the US Department of Housing and Urban Development funded a unique experiment. A total of 4,600 low-income families living in poor areas in public housing participated in the programme.[2] They were randomly divided into three groups. One group received financial assistance (vouchers), practical support and larger housing subsidies to move to more affluent neighbourhoods. A second group received financial support without additional help or guidance. The third group, the control group, received no assistance beyond what they were otherwise eligible for. The experiment, conducted in New York, Los Angeles, Chicago, Boston and Baltimore under the name *Moving to Opportunity for Fair Housing (MTO)*, was carefully monitored and sparked numerous studies (Sanbonmatsu et al. 2011). However, it was difficult to determine the long-term effects on the children involved until now, when they have reached adulthood and entered the workforce.

Only relatively recently, in 2016, did Harvard economists Raj Chetty, Nathanial Hendren and Lawrence Katz publish the first rigorous study of the long-term effects on children. They found strong evidence that moving from poor to middle-income neighbourhoods made a significant difference for children's prospects decades later.

1 See Fölster (2017) for an analysis of how Sweden might have prevented the spread of vulnerable areas.

2 So-called Public Housing Projects, a form of 'social housing'.

However, they also discovered an important caveat: to achieve substantial positive effects, it is crucial for families to move while the children are younger than about 13 years old. If children were older than 13, the effects could even be negative, possibly because it becomes much harder to compensate for earlier deficiencies in the upbringing environment and education. This can place teenagers in a difficult situation. This caveat also explains why earlier studies failed to find significant positive effects of moving on children's educational outcomes.

Children who moved before turning 13, however, were about 30 per cent more likely to attend higher education. On average, their incomes as young adults were also around 30 per cent higher compared to children who did not move. Girls from the families that moved were significantly less likely to become single, young mothers.

These strong results from a true experiment are critically important because they demonstrate something that the otherwise extensive earlier research literature had not been able to convincingly show: that the findings reflect causal relationships rather than hidden differences in the characteristics of people living in different neighbourhoods (see Chetty and Hendren (2015), Chetty et al. (2016) and Fölster (2017) for reviews of the studies).

Much suggests that countries with housing policies that make it relatively easy to find housing have also more easily gained political support for spreading out families with challenges instead of forcing them to concentrate in the least attractive areas. On the other hand, if it is difficult to secure housing, as in Sweden, there is more political resistance if a refugee family is prioritised over a native family that has been on the housing waiting list for a long time.

This link between general housing policies and urban planning that avoids vulnerable areas is illustrated with examples from Switzerland and Germany (Munich). In both cases, while it may also have become difficult to find housing in the most attractive inner-city areas, it is relatively easy to find housing in most other areas.

Low-tax Switzerland has been inspired by the successes of some southern German cities such as Munich and therefore promotes social integration within neighbourhoods. Munich has an immigrant population of 28 per cent, higher than in most European cities. Many arrived as refugees. Yet unemployment is at a record low, and crime rates in Munich are the lowest since the 1980s. In recent years police solved 66 per cent of all crimes and almost all murders. Similarly, Swiss cities such as Zurich and Bern also have low crime rates. These cities show low tolerance for urban decay. Neighbourhoods at risk of becoming vulnerable have been revitalised through deliberate urban planning, a mix of expensive and affordable housing, and plenty of workplaces, even for the smallest businesses. Swiss cities also emphasise the importance of comprehensive projects with measures spanning different policy areas (e.g. urban planning, housing policy, mobility, social integration). These projects are developed and implemented in collaboration with residents and other stakeholders in the neighbourhood, including property owners and real estate industry representatives.

For example, the city of Zurich has supported non-profit housing construction through building cooperatives for over 100 years. Most housing cooperatives voluntarily take on social responsibility and, naturally, also rent apartments to those who are economically or socially disadvantaged. The goal is a balanced mix of household types, ages, incomes, assets, sexes and backgrounds.

It may be challenging to pinpoint exactly why some countries have been quicker to avoid segregated areas. In high-tax Sweden, there has been significant reliance on municipal housing companies, while rent controls and construction bureaucracy have created long housing queues. Against this backdrop, it may have been more challenging to gain support for measures that distribute families with challenges into housing outside vulnerable areas.

In most countries, it is easier to find housing, which also makes it easier to distribute problem families across social housing contracts. Some medium-tax countries such as Germany and Norway have succeeded in adopting housing policies that prevent social problems. However, several low-tax countries such as Switzerland and Japan have also been highly successful in this regard.

This chapter has illustrated the hypothesis that high-tax welfare states can show less interest in preventive measures that could reduce welfare costs in the long term. Most concerning has been how housing policies in countries such as Sweden and France have accelerated the development of vulnerable areas, leading to very high costs for welfare and justice systems. This hypothesis is a heuristic, but it is worth exploring further.

9 LOW-TAX COUNTRIES AVOID 'BOOM-AND-BUST' REFORMS

Another heuristic hypothesis is that voters in high-tax welfare states have been more willing to espouse welfare systems that require much larger tax increases later on. When that proved impossible, the welfare systems had to be pared back at the expense of much political energy and often in combination with a macroeconomic crisis.

During the early phases of welfare state formation economically stable systems were often chosen, such as Bismarck's social insurance scheme, or family policy reforms, such as the introduction of universal child benefits and the expansion of childcare facilities and parental insurance. These partly paid for themselves by encouraging women to enter the labour market. Similarly, the expansion of universal health insurance with income-related sickness benefits and subsidised healthcare followed a European trend that did not necessitate huge tax increases.

In recent decades, however, high-tax countries have in many instances adopted generous welfare systems that economists from the start projected to become unsustainable over time. In high-tax Sweden and France these were overly generous pension systems, generous benefits for unemployment, sick leave and early retirement. As costs rose in these systems, some countries responded by steadily increasing taxes. For example, starting in the early 1970s, tax rates – and particularly marginal taxes – rose faster in Sweden than in most other countries. This marked the beginning of decades of 'boom-and-bust' cycles in Swedish welfare. When the pension system proved unsustainable, it was reformed in 1990/91 with cutbacks and an automatic brake, making the system more robust. But other high-tax countries such as France are still struggling.

Similarly, many countries have had to pare back unemployment and sickness benefits as their scope for higher taxes had been exploited. Typically, countries that today are high-tax countries introduced generous benefits without analysing how incentives might give rise to changing social norms and gradually ever more people on sick leave or unemployment.

A well-documented mechanism arises in the form of so-called benefit traps, where it becomes more financially advantageous to remain unemployed or on sickness benefits than to work. This results from a combination of increased benefits and higher taxes on earned income. Over time, this leads to more individuals relying on benefits and normalising a lifestyle dependent on them.

When costs turn out to be much higher than proponents of generous welfare systems had hoped or expected, a macroeconomic crisis driven by budget deficits and rising public debt can follow. Such a crisis then makes it politically possible to scale back ballooning welfare expenditure. But the costs of such a crisis are usually huge since they entail a recession, unemployment and much individual hardship as people have to adjust their life plans to other circumstances.

Conversely, a significant research literature corroborates that countries that score lower on economic freedom indices, often due to high taxes, fare significantly worse when exposed to a macroeconomic crisis (Callais and Pavlik 2023; Bjørnskov and Rode 2019; Bjørnskov 2016). Recovery also takes longer. This appears to be the case even when the crisis has a completely exogenous cause, such as the Covid pandemic (Geloso and Pavlik 2020; Candela and Geloso 2021).

Other high-tax countries that have been prone to 'boom-and-bust' are Belgium and Italy. Examples of stable low-tax countries are Switzerland and Australia. The latter became more stable after a reform wave during the 1980s.

Sweden had a similar experience. Overly generous welfare systems were introduced in the 1970s and 1980s leading to rapid tax increases and large budget deficits. This contributed significantly to the deep economic crisis of the early 1990s. The crisis provided the political impetus for a complete overhaul of Swedish economic policy in almost all areas. Welfare systems were adapted to more normal European levels. Housing subsidies, which were previously considered a central part of the welfare state, were largely scrapped. Pensions were reformed and lowered. Unemployment benefits and health insurance were tightened. Importantly, fiscal rules were implemented that forced repayment of public debt and avoided large deficits. After these reforms of the 1990s, growth recovered in Sweden, and macroeconomic development has been relatively stable. Also, or as a result, welfare systems have not been subjected to 'boom-and-bust' swings since then.[1]

We do not claim to have established a causal relationship beyond doubt, but a link between a propensity for overly generous welfare systems, high taxes and later bust periods is heuristic and should be further explored.

Patterns of 'boom-and-bust' cycles illustrate that political decision-makers – and ultimately voters – were not particularly concerned with forecasts of future costs when overly generous welfare systems were implemented. Often this occurred despite analyses and calculations warning of potential issues. In some instances, the cost explosion might have been more difficult to predict, for example, due to the systems' influence on social norms. But voters and decision-makers readily assumed that further tax increases would always be possible. This kind of mechanism is a central element of the theory of welfare state crowding out that we develop further in chapter 12.

1 With the exception of an episode of high rates of sick leave in the early 2000s that required tightening of sick leave rules.

10 LOW-TAX COUNTRIES SOMETIMES PURSUE BETTER PUBLIC ASSET GOVERNANCE

Inhabitants of rich countries own significant, partly hidden, public wealth that the state, municipalities and regions neither account for properly nor manage in ways that best benefit the country. A large portion of these assets is used in welfare activities.

Economists have rarely shown much interest in an important mechanism that in reality both drains resources from welfare and hampers overall economic growth, namely, how well public assets are utilised and how wisely investments are made. For welfare, it matters greatly how investments are managed, whether in hospital buildings, roads and electricity infrastructure or in the extensive assets held by public companies.

A large international survey shows that some countries with relatively low taxes also have the most professional governance and management of public assets (Detter and Fölster 2015, 2022; see also Detter and Fölster 2017, 2018). Countries such as Singapore and Australia lead the rankings. Perhaps the awareness that tax increases are not an option increases the motivation to invest public resources more thoughtfully.

According to several studies, Swedish governments, regardless of political affiliation, have almost completely disregarded the societal benefits of infrastructure investments (e.g. Eliasson et al. 2012). According to one estimate, better management that increases the social economic return by just one percentage point could free up resources equal to twice the cost of the entire police force in Sweden (Detter and Fölster 2022).

For companies with private owners, listed on the Stockholm Stock Exchange, governance and management are surrounded by a plethora of boards, company executives, auditors, management consultants, analysts, investors and regulators such as the Financial Supervisory Authority. Analyses and discussions about deals and individuals in these privately owned companies are reported daily.

In contrast, large parts of public wealth are managed non-transparently, passively, almost unprofessionally, or not at all (Detter and Fölster 2017, 2022). Often, this is because valuable assets simply are not accounted for in modern balance sheets or even registered as assets. Democratic governance and oversight barely function when the true value of assets is not visible. As a result, many opportunities to use common wealth to benefit societal development are missed.

Good accounting is a prerequisite, but not a sufficient guarantee, for sound financial management. A mountain of unnecessary costs is also growing due to neglected maintenance, such as of railways or water supplies. Mismanagement of the electricity infrastructure alone causes hundreds of billions in unnecessary societal costs. Through a series of reforms, insights from corporate governance in private companies could be adopted, increasing value creation to benefit everyone.

Key to better public wealth management is professional accounting of assets, adhering to at least the same standards required of private companies. New Zealand's public financial system, reformed over 30 years ago, serves as a model. In this modern system, all assets are regularly accounted for based on market value or replacement cost. Additionally, independent efficiency audits of asset management are conducted in local governments by National Audit Offices. So far, many high-tax countries have failed to implement similar governance reforms.

Some countries, in particular low-tax countries, have had excellent experiences managing state-owned companies through holding companies or similar structures, with low-tax Singapore being a leader and role model. Similarly, low-tax Australia and New Zealand could serve as models for others to adopt an analytical unit similar to 'Infrastructure Australia', reporting directly to parliament. This unit would establish a priority list of investments and analyse needs and profitability. The operational part of the Transport Administration would then be converted into a state-owned company under the Ministry of Finance or, preferably, an independent holding company that could more flexibly procure and co-invest with other stakeholders. Norway has successfully implemented a similar transformation.

One reason some low-tax countries perform better in several welfare aspects than Sweden may be that economically smarter governance of public assets can unlock significant potential for welfare.

11 LOW-TAX COUNTRIES PROVIDE SOCIAL PROTECTION WITH LOWER TRANSFERS BUT MORE PREFUNDED SAVINGS

A large share of welfare costs consists of social insurance and benefit systems, which are often claimed to require high taxes. However, countries with low taxes have found various ways to ensure that people with low incomes also have a safety net. In low-tax countries that have been less successful in welfare quality, such as the US, there are usually some tax-funded transfers supplemented by means-tested social assistance, housing benefits and in-kind support (such as food stamps).

In the more successful low-tax countries, income security has instead been built by introducing or encouraging systems that replace tax-funded transfers with elements of mandatory and voluntary individual savings. Even high-tax Sweden has moved slightly in this direction after its crisis in the early 1990s. The purely tax-funded pension system was replaced with a partly prefunded one, which has increasingly taken on the characteristics of a basic safety net, with minimal differentiation between those who have worked their entire lives and those who have not. Instead, this differentiation is now created through savings in the form of occupational pensions, private pension savings and mandatory individual pension savings.

A relatively extensive body of research has examined the consequences of moving towards systems with savings components, even applied to unemployment benefits and other social insurances. Some of the world's most renowned economists have studied this issue and drawn positive conclusions, including both market-liberal economists such as the late Harvard Professor Martin Feldstein, and those with a penchant for redistribution, such as Nobel laureate Professor Joseph Stiglitz (Feldstein 1974).

The roots of this body of research lie in discussions about funded versus unfunded pension systems. Martin Feldstein, as early as the 1970s, studied how funded pension accounts impact wealth accumulation.

One conclusion from econometric studies in the US was that unfunded public pensions, similar to Social Security, reduce private savings by 30–50 per cent. An unfunded system is essentially a promise that future generations will pay taxes to finance the promised pensions. Since less is saved in real terms, less is also invested, resulting in a real loss of growth and income (Feldstein 1998).

This research was further developed in the 1990s. It showed that the growth-inhibiting effects of unfunded social insurance systems are due to:

(a) a portion of the contributions acting as a tax that does not provide an expected benefit in the form of higher future pensions, thus reducing labour supply, and

(b) lower levels of savings and investment.

Increasing the degree of funding in pensions would therefore reduce both of these growth-inhibiting effects. These ideas also gained traction in Sweden, primarily through increased funding levels in many occupational pensions, as well as the introduction of a funded component in the public pension system.

Some countries have restructured their social insurance systems to focus on lifetime earnings rather than basing benefits on the most recently paid salary. Such systems can significantly reduce marginal effects in the tax system.

Globally, social security systems with savings elements have made significant progress. Around 20 countries have implemented such systems, sometimes on a small scale. Singapore, the pioneer in this area, has had positive experiences with its comprehensive pension savings programme combined with systems that include both savings and insurance elements. The system is known as the Central Provident Fund (CPF) (see, for example, Central Provident Fund Board 2015). Established in 1955 by the British colonial government, it originally served solely as a pension scheme. Initially, employers and employees each contributed 5 per cent of wages to the employee's individual account in the central fund. The system was retained after Singapore's independence in 1959 and its scope expanded significantly over time.

Today, employers and employees each contribute approximately 20 per cent of wage costs, though the exact percentages have varied. The funds are allocated to each employee's three separate CPF accounts approximately as follows:

1. Ordinary Account (CPF-OA). The largest portion is deposited here. These funds can be used for housing purchases, investments in stocks, purchasing insurance, and more. The account can also finance the individual's or their children's post-secondary education or be transferred to support parents who may not have substantial CPF savings of their own. After retirement this account finances a pension.
2. Medisave Account. A smaller portion, introduced in 1984, is deposited here. This account is used to cover the individual's or their family members' medical expenses and certain vaccinations.
3. Special Account. Around 4 per cent of the contribution is directed to this account, which is reserved for basic pensions and emergencies.

The system includes several safety net elements for those who cannot save enough or afford healthcare costs.

Singapore has used this approach to enable large groups of low-income earners to purchase homes, allowing them to participate in wealth growth that would otherwise be limited to wealthier individuals.

In sum, successful low-tax countries rely to a greater extent on income security through prefunded savings that can be individual and voluntary, individual and mandatory within public systems, or part of collective bargaining agreements and administered by employers or financial institutions they cooperate with.

12 WELFARE STATE CROWDING OUT

The foregoing chapters have presented a collection of observations that illustrate why high-tax countries no longer dominate the welfare quality leagues. Based on these examples this section formulates a *theory of welfare state crowding out* which structures the mechanisms by which countries with higher tax burdens fail to achieve the best welfare outcomes.

Seven hundred years ago, the Tunisian economist and social scientist Ibn Khaldun had already laid the foundations for the understanding that states often, in connection with expansion towards higher tax levels, precipitated displacement of work, investment and talent. An expanding public sector at some point through excessive taxation crowds out economic activity in the private sector, shrinking the tax base. Arthur Laffer then developed the theory further, in his famous napkin sketch during a dinner. The result is the Laffer curve (which we could also call Laffer–Khaldun curve), which shows the link between tax level and tax revenue (for a summary of Ibn Khaldun's works, see Sanandaji 2018). It shows how taxes crowd out economic growth. Slower growth also dampens wage increases. Therefore, slower growth may not make it more difficult to employ a share of the population in welfare services, but it does make it more difficult to finance investments and items such as medicines that are often imported.

In 2010, a study by Mathias Trabandt and Harald Uhlig published by the European Central Bank found that many European countries were close to or at the top of the Laffer curve in terms of capital taxation, but also labour taxation (Trabandt and Uhlig 2010). This reflects a situation in which taxation is so damaging to the economy, that on the margin it even crowds out tax revenues.

The marginal effects can be even stronger. In Sweden there was an extensive public debate on 'the protection tax' ('värnskatten'), a supposedly temporary 5 per cent extra top marginal tax for high-income earners. This tax was introduced in 1995 and abolished in 2020 during a social democratic government. The Ministry of Finance estimated before the reform that the abolition of the tax would probably be self-financing (Swedish Finance Department 2019; see also Confederation of Swedish Enterprise 2024). These results are important for the understanding of welfare state crowding out.

Another mechanism for how welfare services crowd out other sectors of the economy is Baumol's cost disease. Willian Baumol showed that if a large part of the economy, such as public welfare services, does not achieve the same productivity growth rate as other industries (because they are labour intensive), they will be increasingly difficult to finance (Baumol 1990). The reason is that wages in welfare services have to be raised roughly at the same rate as in other sectors of the economy. Without a commensurate productivity increase, a country has to accept declining levels of welfare services relative to other consumption. Alternatively, it has to shift an increasing share of national income to financing of welfare.

Our analysis and cases add additional mechanisms of how welfare state generosity not only crowds out other sectors of the economy but actually cannibalises its own core functions and over time leads to a deterioration of welfare quality and standards.

One reason seems to be that efficiency may appear less important to people in a country where the perception is that taxes can always be raised further. Such a perception also raises the expectations of what the welfare state should provide. For example, one study finds that the French are least satisfied with their social protection even though they objectively receive more than respondents in comparison countries (OECD 2024). Such an attitude can also be self-reinforcing. People who expect generous welfare state provisions in the future are likely to save less or prepare themselves for calamities. As a result, they will be objectively less resilient, and more adamant in their demands for support in times of need. The UK is a good example, having been until recently a low-tax country, according to the analysis used in this book (using average outcomes since 2010). During the past few years, however, the tax level has been raised above 35 per cent of GDP. As taxes and public expenditure rise, there is increased demand for more public expenditure. At the same time, public expenditure, as well as the increased taxes, are crowding out private sector economic activity, and thus shrinking the tax base.

Another mechanism behind the relative deterioration of the welfare capacity of high-tax countries may be that, over time, countries with higher taxes experience growing difficulties in paring cost-driving factors. Examples of this are swelling bureaucracy, an increasing demographic burden and increasing demands that are sometimes referred to as Wagner's law. Wagner's law stipulates that rising incomes generate a relatively greater demand for public services than for private ones.

In countries where many believe that the scope for future taxes is huge, Baumol's law and Wagner's law are often described as natural laws that cannot be altered. In reality, Wagner's law has always been more of a political ambition than a natural law. In the end there is a budget restriction for welfare spending regardless of public demand. As far as Baumol's law is concerned, many have overlooked the fact that the productivity growth rate in welfare services appears lower than it actually is, since the benefits of new medical treatments and other technological advances in welfare services are not measured in national accounts.

Increasing demand for welfare services can also result from welfare systems themselves changing social norms in a cost-driving manner (see also Sanandaji and Heller Sahlgren 2022). Lindbeck (2008a; see also 2008b) and Ljunge (2012), for example, find evidence that social norms surrounding security systems, particularly health insurance, have changed over time. As the welfare system has expanded and more people have become recipients of benefits, acceptance of dependency on the system for livelihood has increased. Consequently, they also see an increased risk of system overutilisation. It was no coincidence that research on the shift in social norms gained momentum after the unprecedented rise in sick leave that Sweden experienced in the early 2000s, which for a period rendered Swedes the highest rate of sick leave in the world, even though objectively they were among the healthiest people.

Expectations and attitudes within a population also affect political and administrative strategies. In the research literature, it emerges that the welfare system's performance in relation to its efforts – its productivity – has weakened in recent years in several high-tax countries. For example, Sweden's public expenditures yield, in international comparison, poor results per invested krona. A series of new research reports, for example, compare public expenditures to an index of achieved outcomes, such as the quality of education, healthcare, infrastructure or income distribution and the level of corruption (see, for example, Afonso et al. 2020). In some of these areas, Sweden has less favourable results, in others very good ones, but they are achieved with unusually high public expenditures. Per invested krona, the results are poor compared to many other countries.

The exact mechanisms for how high-tax countries may slack when it comes to efficiency are hard to determine. It could be that politicians and administrators are more willing to cut corners or agree to bad compromises when they believe that taxes can be further raised. They may be more willing to give in to demands, for example, from labour unions, that affect efficiency negatively. One interesting mechanism is also that they may be less interested in institutions that discipline decision-making to deliver more efficient outcomes.

For example, Sweden only implemented reforms after the deep crisis in the early 1990s, such as a semi-independent oversight of the pension system, with automatic pension cuts if revenues were calculated to fall short of expenditures over coming decades. In a similar vein, a fiscal framework was introduced that mitigated against budget deficits except during recessions.

Some successful low-tax countries have gone much further. For example, New Zealand has introduced a modern accounting system in its public sector, based on double-entry bookkeeping and accrual accounting with fair valuation of assets, where the balance sheet is linked to the budget. This provides a much-needed basis for governance of public assets that most countries lack. The reach of government accounting bodies has been extended to local government (Detter and Fölster 2015).

Both New Zealand and Australia have introduced semi-independent bodies such as 'Infrastructure Australia' that calculate costs and benefits and monitor infrastructure investments (Detter and Fölster 2022).

All in all, high-tax countries thus have significant difficulties in managing the automatic cost-driving factors that all countries are exposed to. In countries where welfare is mainly financed by taxes, this quickly inflates taxes to levels that exact a high price for growth. At some point taxes and public expenditure even crowd out welfare outcomes, not least for unemployment and education, since overly generous welfare states create poverty traps and reduce the incentives for education.

Can welfare state crowding out be reversed?

This systematic comparison of 23 developed economies shows that some countries with lower tax burdens achieve better welfare outcomes and faster economic growth. Countries with lower tax burdens manage to maintain lower unemployment rates, particularly among the less educated, but also among those with medium and high levels of education. These countries also achieve significantly better school outcomes in PISA subjects such as mathematics, reading comprehension and science.

High taxes stifle prosperity during periods of population growth, and in times of stagnant or shrinking populations it is even more important to strive for growing economies. As the share of working-age adults declines, with aging populations and falling birth rates, it will become increasingly important to rely on workfare rather than welfare. It is likewise vital to strengthen the norms of work, welfare and responsibility of the young generation. Economic policies of limited government and lower taxation levels create incentives, not only for work but also for studying with grit in school, aiming to achieve future career success. The welfare state crowding out theory is relevant to understanding prosperity, education, health and exclusion in advanced economies.

Looking to the future, these considerations become even more critical. A focus on efficiency will make it easier to manage increasing cost pressures resulting from demographic changes, pandemics and labour shortages. The strain on welfare systems will only intensify as most countries' populations are aging. This will lead to greater demand for healthcare and elderly care. Additionally, there will be a growing shortage of personnel for public welfare services. These factors place immense pressure on welfare funding. Without a well-thought-out strategy, the patterns of recent decades – where expansive systems suddenly face austerity measures – will persist, driving more to seek private alternatives such as personal savings, insurance and fully privatised services.

What can be learned from the mechanisms that allow some low-tax countries to excel in welfare delivery despite smaller tax revenues? In summary, a few key insights relevant for high-tax welfare states stand out.

Prevention of social problems. Some low-tax countries have been more successful in preventing social problems, particularly those that heavily burden welfare systems, such as crime and social challenges.

Efficient organisation of welfare. Many low-tax countries ensure that welfare services are organised efficiently. A recurring theme in examples from sectors like healthcare and elderly care is encouraging competition between different organisational models and payment structures.

Building resilience in individuals. Successful low-tax countries have made people more resilient during crises.

Instead of many being entirely dependent on public transfers that can be cut at short notice during a crisis, these countries have systems with a greater emphasis on personal savings and self-reliance.

Economic growth through lower taxes. Low-tax countries have leveraged the growth-stimulating effects of lower taxes. Many of these nations have also promoted economic growth more effectively through reduced bureaucracy, smarter energy policies and wiser public investments.

All these principles are obviously easier when a large share of the population realises that the future cannot be secured for high-tax welfare states and the rest of Europe by focusing on taxing past wealth instead of creating new prosperity. Without reforms toward a lower tax burden, welfare, growth and demographic challenges are all likely to become harder to manage.

Reforming towards a lower tax burden is not a guarantee of success in these challenges, but – with well-designed policies, experience and data support – it can be part of the solution. In many cases institutions can also be designed to help in this task, such as better government accounting practices, more independent review systems and governance of pension systems or infrastructure, as well as opening up welfare services to well-designed competition. With smart policy development, high-tax welfare states can achieve better future growth, welfare and demographics – through a transition to a low-tax model.

REFERENCES

Afonso, A. and Jalles, J. T. (2014) Fiscal composition and long-term growth. *Applied Economics* 46(3): 349–58.

Afonso, A., Jalles, J. T. and Venâncio, A. (2020) Government spending efficiency, measurement and applications: a cross country efficiency dataset. EconPol Working Paper 50, ifo Institute, Leibniz Institute for Economic Research at the University of Munich.

Allemani, C. et al. (2018) Global surveillance of trends in cancer survival 2000–14 (CONCORD-3): analysis of individual records for 37 513 025 patients diagnosed with one of 18 cancers from 322 population-based registries in 71 countries. *The Lancet* 391(10125): 1023–75.

Baumol, W. J. (1990) Entrepreneurship: productive, unproductive and destructive. *Journal of Political Economy* 98(5): 893–921.

Bergh, A. and Bjørnskov, C. (2021) Does economic freedom boost growth for everyone? *Kyklos* 74(2): 170–86.

Bergh, A. and Henrekson, M. (2011) Government size and growth: a survey and interpretation of the evidence. *Journal of Economic Surveys* 25(5): 872–97.

Bergh, A. and Henrekson, M. (2016) Government size and growth: a rejoinder. *Journal of Economic Surveys* 30(2): 393–96.

Bjornberg, A. and Phang, A. Y. (2019) *Euro Health Consumer Index 2018*. Health Consumer Powerhouse.

Bjørnskov, C. (2016) Economic freedom and economic crises. *European Journal of Political Economy* 45(S): 11–23.

Bjørnskov, C. and Rode, M. (2019) Crisis, ideology, and interventionist policy ratchets. *Political Studies* 67(4): 815–33.

Blix, M. and Jordahl, H. (2021) *Privatizing Welfare Services: Lessons from the Swedish Experiment.* Oxford University Press.

Callais, J. T. and Pavlik, J. B. (2023) Does economic freedom lighten the blow? Evidence from the great recession in the United States. *Economics of Governance* 24: 357–98.

Candela, R. A. and Geloso, V. (2021) Economic freedom, pandemics, and robust political economy. *Southern Economic Journal* 87(4): 1250–66.

Central Provident Fund Board (2015) *Annual Report 2015.* Singapore.

Chetty, R. and Hendren, N. (2015) *The Impacts of Neighborhoods on Intergenerational Mobility: Childhood Exposure Effects and County-Level Estimates.* Cambridge, MA: Harvard University and the National Bureau for Economic Research.

Chetty, R., Hendren, N. and Katz, L. F. (2016) The effects of exposure to better neighborhoods on children: new evidence from the moving to opportunity experiment. *American Economic Review* 106(4): 855–902.

Confederation of Swedish Enterprise (2024) Skatteeffekter av värnskattens avskaffande. Prememoria by Fredrik Carlgren, 22 April 2024.

Dean, J. and Geloso, V. (2022) Economic freedom improves income mobility: evidence from Canadian provinces, 1982–2018. *Journal of Institutional Economics* 18(5): 807–26.

Detter, D. and Fölster, S. (2015) *The Public Wealth of Nations.* London: Palgrave Macmillan.

Detter, D. and Fölster, S. (2017) *The Public Wealth of Cities*. Washington, DC: Brookings Institution.

Detter, D. and Fölster, S. (2018) Unlocking public wealth, governments could do a better job managing their assets. IMF F&D Magazine.

Detter, D. and Fölster, S. (2022) *Konsten att Tappa Bort 4 000 Miljarder Kronor*. Stockholm: Samhällsförlaget.

Economist, The (2013) Special report: the Nordic countries.

Eliasson, J., Börjesson, M., Odeck, J. and Welde, M. (2015) Does benefit–cost efficiency influence transport investment decisions? *Journal of Transport Economics and Policy* 49(3): 377–96.

Esping-Andersen, G. (1990) *The Three Worlds of Welfare Capitalism*. Cambridge: Polity Press.

Feldstein, M. (1974) Social security, induced retirement and aggregate capital accumulation. *Journal of Political Economy* 82(5): 905–26.

Feldstein, M. (1998) *Privatizing Social Security*. University of Chicago Press.

Finanspolitiska Rådet (2024) Economic inequality in Sweden: an overview of facts and future challenges. Särskilda studier från Finanspolitiska Rådet 2024/1, Stockholm.

Fölster, S. (2017) Den inkluderande staden: stadsutveckling i kommuners gränstrakter med exemplet Järva Storstad. Stockholm.

Fölster, S. and Sanandaji, N. (2023) *Reformer för Politiker som vill bli Återvalda*. Stockholm: Timbro.

Fölster, S. and Sanandaji, N. (2024) *Lågskatteländer Toppar Välfärdsligan: Medan Högskatteländer Tappar*. Stockholm: Skattebetalarnas Förening.

Forum för Health Policy (2017) *Vad kan Sverige lära av Nederländerna och Schweiz?* Stockholm.

Geloso, V. (2023) What accounts for America's life expectancy gap? The Daily Economy, 26 May 2023, American Institute for Economic Research (https://thedailyeconomy.org/article/what-accounts-for-americas-life-expectancy-gap/).

Geloso, V. and Pavlik, J. (2020) Economic freedom and the economic consequences of the 1918 pandemic. *Contemporary Economic Policy* 39(2): 255–63.

Hanushek, E. A. (1994) Money might matter somewhere: a response to Hedges, Laine, and Greenwald. *Educational Researcher* 23(4): 5–8.

Kreier, R. and Zweifel, P. (2010) Health insurance in Switzerland: a closer look at a system often offered as a model for the United States. *Hofstra L. Rev.* 39: 89.

Lindbeck, A. (2008a) Sociala normer och socialförsäkringar: teori och svenska erfarenheter. *Ekonomisk Debatt* 36(6): 17–30.

Lindbeck, A. (2008b) Prospects for the welfare state. IFN Working Paper 731.

Ljunge, M. (2012) The spirit of the welfare state? Adaptation in the demand for social insurance. *Journal of Human Capital* 6(3): 187–223.

Lundbäck, M. (2022) Schweiz sjukvårdssystem: effektiva lösningar utan central styrning. Ratioakademiens sjukvårdsprojekt nr. 4, Ratio, Stockholm (https://ratio.se/publikationer/schweiz-sjukvardssystem-effektiva-losningar-utan-central-styrning).

Lundberg, J. and Norell, J. (2020). Taxes, benefits and labour force participation: a survey of the quasi-experimental literature. *Journal of the Finnish Economic Association* 1.1: 60–77.

Makin, A. J., Pearce, J. and Ratnasiri, S. (2019) The optimal size of government in Australia. *Economic Analysis and Policy* 62: 27–36.

Niemietz, K. (2024) The denationalisation of healthcare: how to replace the NHS with a social health insurance system. IEA Discussion Paper 128 (https://iea.org.uk/publications/the-denationalisation-of-healthcare/). London: Institute of Economic Affairs.

OECD (2011) Taxation and employment. OECD Tax Policy Studies, October 2011, Paris: OECD.

OECD (2023) *Health at a Glance 2023*, Country Note Sweden. Paris: OECD

OECD (2024) *Content or Discontent? Perceptions of Social Protection in France, Germany and the United Kingdom*. Paris: OECD (https://doi.org/10.1787/57b4436c-en).

Roine, J. and Waldenström, D. (2011) On the role of capital gains in Swedish income inequality. *Review of Income and Wealth* 58(3): 569–87.

Sanandaji, N. (2015) *Scandinavian Unexceptionalism: Culture, Markets and the Failure of Third-Way Socialism*. London: Institute of Economic Affairs.

Sanandaji, N. (2018) *The Birthplace of Capitalism: The Middle East*. Timbro.

Sanandaji, N. and Heller Sahlgren, G. (2022) *Normboken: Vad spelar normer for roll och hur har det utvecklats över tid?* Vulkan.

Sanbonmatsu, L., Katz, L. F., Ludwig, J., Gennetian, L. A., Duncan, G. J., Kessler, R. C. and Lindau, S. T. (2011) *Moving to Opportunity for Fair Housing Demonstration Program: Final Impacts Evaluation*. National Bureau of Economic Research.

Scully, G. W. (2003) Optimal taxation, economic growth and income inequality. *Public Choice* 115(3): 299–312.

Shellenberger, M. (2021) *San Fransicko: Why Progressives Ruin Cities*. Harper.

Swedish Finance Department (2019) Budgetpropositionen för 2020, Regeringens proposition 2019/20:1, Finansdepartementet.

Trabandt, M. and Uhlig, H. (2010) How far are we from the slippery slope? The Laffer curve revisited. Working Paper 1174, European Central Bank.

ABOUT THE IEA

The Institute of Economic Affairs is a research and educational charity (No. CC 235 351). Its mission is to improve understanding of the fundamental institutions of a free society by analysing and expounding the role of markets in solving economic and social problems.

The IEA achieves its mission through:

- a high-quality publishing programme
- conferences, seminars, lectures and other events
- outreach to school and university students
- appearances across print, broadcast and digital media

The IEA, established in 1955 by the late Sir Antony Fisher, is an educational charity, not a political organisation. It is independent of any political party or group and does not carry on activities intended to affect support for any political party or candidate in any election or referendum, or at any other time. It is financed by sales of publications, conference fees and voluntary donations.

In addition to its main series of publications, the IEA publishes the academic journal *Economic Affairs* in partnership with the University of Buckingham.

The IEA is aided in its work by an Academic Advisory Council and a panel of Honorary Fellows. Together with other academics, they review prospective IEA publications, their comments being passed on anonymously to authors. All IEA papers are therefore subject to the same rigorous, independent refereeing process as used by leading academic journals.

IEA publications are often used in classrooms and incorporated into school and university courses. They are also sold throughout the world and often translated and reprinted. The IEA supports and works with a global network of like-minded organisations, through its Initiative for African Trade and Prosperity, EPICENTER and other international programmes.

Views expressed in the IEA's publications are those of the authors, not those of the Institute (which has no corporate view), its Managing Trustees, Academic Advisory Council members or senior staff. Members of the Institute's Academic Advisory Council, Honorary Fellows, Trustees and Staff are listed on the following page.

The Institute gratefully acknowledges financial support for its publications programme and other work from a generous benefaction by the late Professor Ronald Coase.

The Institute of Economic Affairs
2 Lord North Street, Westminster, London SW1P 3LB
Tel: 020 7799 8900
Email: iea@iea.org.uk
Web: iea.org.uk

Other books recently published by the IEA include:

Raising the Roof: How to Solve the United Kingdom's Housing Crisis
Edited by Jacob Rees-Mogg and Radomir Tylecote
ISBN 978-0-255-36782-0; £12.50

How Many Light Bulbs Does It Take to Change the World?
Matt Ridley and Stephen Davies
ISBN 978-0-255-36785-1; £10.00

The Henry Fords of Healthcare … Lessons the West Can Learn from the East
Nima Sanandaji
ISBN 978-0-255-36788-2; £10.00

An Introduction to Entrepreneurship
Eamonn Butler
ISBN 978-0-255-36794-3; £12.50

An Introduction to Democracy
Eamonn Butler
ISBN 978-0-255-36797-4; £12.50

Having Your Say: Threats to Free Speech in the 21st Century
Edited by J. R. Shackleton
ISBN 978-0-255-36800-1; £17.50

The Sharing Economy: Its Pitfalls and Promises
Michael C. Munger
ISBN 978-0-255-36791-2; £12.50

An Introduction to Trade and Globalisation
Eamonn Butler
ISBN 978-0-255-36803-2; £12.50

Why Free Speech Matters
Jamie Whyte
ISBN 978-0-255-36806-3; £10.00

The People Paradox: Does the World Have Too Many or Too Few People?
Steven E. Landsburg and Stephen Davies
ISBN 978-0-255-36809-4; £10.00

An Introduction to Economic Inequality
Eamonn Butler
ISBN 978-0-255-36815-5; £10.00

Carbon Conundrum: How to Save Climate Change Policy from Government Failure
Philip Booth and Carlo Stagnaro
ISBN 978-0-255-36812-4; £12.50

Scaling the Heights: Thought Leadership, Liberal Values and the History of The Mont Pelerin Society
Eamonn Butler
ISBN 978-0-255-36818-6; £10.00

Faith in Markets? Abrahamic Religions and Economics
Edited by Benedikt Koehler
ISBN 978-0-255-36824-7; £17.50

Human Nature and World Affairs: An Introduction to Classical Liberalism and International Relations Theory
Edwin van de Haar
ISBN 978-0-255-36827-8; £15.00

The Experience of Free Banking
Edited by Kevin Dowd
ISBN 978-0-255-36830-8; £25.00

Apocalypse Next: The Economics of Global Catastrophic Risks
Stephen Davies
ISBN 978-0-255-36821-6; £17.50

New Paternalism Meets Older Wisdom: Looking to Smith and Hume on Rationality, Welfare and Behavioural Economics
Erik W. Matson
ISBN 978-0-255-36833-9; £12.50

An Introduction to Taxation
Eamonn Butler
ISBN 978-0-255-36836-0; £12.50

Imperial Measurement: A Cost–Benefit Analysis of Western Colonialism
Kristian Niemietz
ISBN 978-0-255-36839-1; £10.00

The Quantity Theory of Money: A New Restatement
Tim Congdon
ISBN 978-0-255-36842-1; £15.00

Unions Resurgent? The Past, Present and Uncertain Future of Trade Unions in Britain
J. R. Shackleton
ISBN 978-0-255-36845-2; £15.00

An Introduction to Schools of Economic Thought
Eamonn Butler
ISBN 978-0-255-36848-3; £12.50

Other IEA publications

Comprehensive information on other publications and the wider work of the IEA can be found at www.iea.org.uk. To order any publication please see below.

Personal customers

Orders from personal customers should be directed to the IEA:

IEA
2 Lord North Street
Westminster
London SW1P 3LB
Tel: 020 7799 8911
Email: accounts@iea.org.uk

Trade customers

All orders from the book trade should be directed to the IEA's distributor:

Ingram Publisher Services UK
1 Deltic Avenue
Rooksley
Milton Keynes MK13 8LD
Tel: 01752 202301
Email: ipsuk.orders@ingramcontent.com

IEA subscriptions

The IEA offers a subscription service. For £350 a year, UK-based subscribers will receive every book the IEA publishes along with invitations to IEA events – while also supporting the IEA's charitable mission. You can subscribe online by becoming a 'Founding Insider' at insider.iea.org.uk. Otherwise, please contact:

Subscriptions
IEA
2 Lord North Street
Westminster
London SW1P 3LB
Tel: 020 7799 8911
Email: accounts@iea.org.uk